An Enlightened Philosophy

Can an atheist believe anything?

An Enlightened Philosophy

Can an atheist believe anything?

Geoff Crocker

BOOKS

Winchester, UK
Washington, USA

First published by O-Books, 2010
O Books is an imprint of John Hunt Publishing Ltd., The Bothy, Deershot Lodge, Park Lane, Ropley,
Hants, SO24 0BE, UK
office1@o-books.net
www.o-books.com

For distributor details and how to order please visit the 'Ordering' section on our website.

Text copyright Geoff Crocker 2010

ISBN: 978 1 84694 424 6

A CIP catalogue record for this book is available from the British Library.

Design: Stuart Davies

Printed in the UK by CPI Antony Rowe
Printed in the USA by Offset Paperback Mfrs, Inc

We operate a distinctive and ethical publishing philosophy in all
areas of its business, from its global network of authors to
production and worldwide distribution.

CONTENTS

Geoff Crocker seeks to steer a pathway between traditional theistic religion and other non-rationalistic approaches whilst refusing to settle for the nihilism and amorality implicit in much postmodern culture and thought. He sees usefulness in classical religious myths to augment a pure rationalism, providing enrichment and sustenance to the human search for value and ethics. His criticisms of the Church may be bruising for some Christians to read, but his argument also cuts in an opposite direction to challenge a value-free postmodernism or neo-rationalism and their application in 'the Market' and popular attitudes to moral discourse. Here is a new and clear voice in popular philosophy which deserves a hearing by religious and non-religious readers seeking to make sense of our world today.

Paul Roberts, Dean of Non-residential Training, St Michael's College, Llandaff, Cardiff

This is a book to leave you reeling, provoked - and hopeful. Geoff Crocker embraces the death of God, but not the simplistic mantras of Dawkins-style 'new' atheism. Advocating nothing less than a synthesis of the sacred and the secular, he finds a divine power in religious myth even when its supernatural content is stripped away. Make no mistake: this book pulls no punches in its critique of the church, and many will want to argue with its bold claims. But ultimately this is a work of profoundly spiritual hope, nothing less than a philosophy of life for disenchanted times.

Steven Shakespeare, Lecturer in Philosophy, Liverpool Hope University

Geoff Crocker brings a fresh voice to the God debate, arguing that Biblical mythology and critical thinking need not be enemies. Eloquent and persuasive.

David Boulton, Author of *The Trouble with God* and *Who on Earth was Jesus?*

Geoff Crocker embarks on a noble project indeed as he attempts to synthesise from both ends of the contemporary theistic/atheistic spectrum the moral framework for a viable 21st century living model.

Although this timely volume basically critiques the writings of others (the author's personal selection) Geoff's own voice frequently breaks out to challenge his readers with undisguised passion. His analysis of the western zeitgeist rings true and he touches some interesting areas of secular and religious life.

For lively and open-minded folk, particularly those who can't find the time to digest 'in the original' the plethora of philosophical rethinking currently hitting the shelves, the book may act as a useful prompt to revisit their trusty traditional moral compass - to find it needs considerable adjustment for journeying in a fast-moving new century.

Penny Mawdsley

Faith and Atheism – a possible synthesis?

Think back. It's 2009. The world seems suddenly very insecure, unusually unsure of itself. The Brave New World feels hesitant, the NICE decade of non-inflationary constant expansion has come to an end. Banks are collapsing, businesses going bankrupt, unemployment rising. The successful 'Free Markets and Social Democracy' formula in which much of the world had put its trust now seems less reliable. The post modern profile of humanity as consumer is fading. This coincides with continuation of the long term erosion of any belief system. Nietzsche long ago declared God to be dead. Contemporary populist writers like Richard Dawkins are confident that there is no God and take out bus adverts to say so. Atheism is on the attack and the church is in retreat, either busying itself with internal squabbles about sexuality and gender, or with marginal attempts to engage the culture in pubs, though even there no one is quite sure what message it wants to convey. Church leaders like Richard Holloway or John Spong who seek to re-interpret its message are marginalised.

The antipathy between culture and church has a long history. Roy Porter in his 'Flesh in the Age of Reason' traces the development of the philosophical questioning of the existence of a separate soul. The Enlightenment challenged fearful spiritual interpretations and replaced them with logical explanations, a process described in Louis Dupre's 'Enlightenment and the Intellectual Foundations of Modern Culture'. In cosmology Copernicus and Galileo were proved right. In medicine too, by harnessing reason and logic for explanation and application, modernity succeeded where religion had failed. Through recurrent epidemics of bubonic plague, cholera, influenza, typhus and smallpox, religion offered no solution other than meek acceptance of fate, whereas the new medicines really did heal diseases, and hygiene really did prevent them. Rational scientific research discovered physical, chemical and biological interactions and engineered them into technologies to increase economic provision. Human lifestyles and possibility flourished even though for many, human realities remained grim. The Enlightenment had placed logic on the throne and challenged feudal power on which the church had relied. Technology became a greater determinant of human life than God. All this applies to the western world, or the world defined by the dominance of Enlightenment modernity. Meanwhile in Islamic cultures religion still prevails and dominates, in India like everything else it co-exists, in China it is suppressed, in America it has largely become part of consumerist culture.

In Europe, the cradle of the Enlightenment, the church and religion have decisively lost this one sided battle. But one sided outcomes imply loss of content. The losing side might have had something of value to say. Classic dialectics forges thesis with antithesis to gain an improved synthesis. Current atheist populism destroys religious belief but offers no philosophy to replace it. It is nihilistic. This book admits the atheist hypothesis, but at the same time retains elements from religion where they can add value, although they will require substantial re-interpretation from the classical religious view.

The main synthesis

The main synthesis developed in this book is between a recognition of **meaningful metaphysics** in philosophy with a recognition of the **power of myth** in religion.

Even if there is no God and no separate human soul, even if everything is ultimately physical, even so a metaphysical still exists. Or it is at least a workable, useful and credible hypothesis that it is 'as if' a metaphysical exists. It may be entirely hosted by and dependent on the physical, but this does not deny its existence, only its independence. By metaphysical I do not mean the impenetrable discussions of Aristotlean philosophers about categories and qualia, but more immediate familiar metaphysicals such as ideas, feelings, group dynamics, institutions and totalities. An idea does need to be registered in a physical brain or recorded in text form on physical paper or physical computer disk, and in this sense it is physical or physically dependent. An idea is incapable of existence independently of the brain that generates it or the medium that hosts it. But curiously the idea can transfer its host medium with ease. It can be in a brain cell or neuron complex one minute, formulated by the tongue to be conveyed in the sound waves of speech the next, received in the ear drum and decoded into a second brain, written on paper, typed onto a computer disk, sent over the Internet. It can replicate itself an infinite number of times in an instant of time into millions of hosts. This multiplication of the idea in location occurs with no matching increase in physicality of the idea, no increase in mass, thus proving its metaphysical reality. It can mutate by encounter with other ideas. Although this mutation can only take place in a human brain, the modified idea can then edit itself back into its endless number of physical hosts. It can powerfully drive physical action and interpersonal interaction. A similar argument can be developed using feelings and emotions. They also only exist in a physical host, and can even be felt physically in heart or gut, but nevertheless have metaphysical significance.

Without the physical there would be no ideas, but ideas themselves are metaphysical. The same is true of life. The molecular physicality of a dead body and a living body is very similar, with that of a sleeping body somewhere in between. The

3

only difference is the lack of cell and organ movement, presumably due to some physical electro-chemical. But the metaphysical difference is huge – not only ideas which exist in life but not in death, but also the personality with all its capabilities, its hopes and fears, its loves and hates, its creative potential - and that metaphysic is life. Life is a metaphysic.

No-one disputes the need for physical life to be supported and enabled with food, clothing, shelter and all the consumer products made available by advanced technology. The need, or at least the creative scope for provision, nurture and management of the metaphysical is therefore similarly evident. Here is where religion has a lost role. I will argue that religion which is doctrine, phenomena or ritual is inadequate and meaningless compared to religion which is interpreted more powerfully as myth. Myth has a history of being despised as a weak word for a weak idea. It can even mean simply 'untrue' in common speech. But myth classically understood offers huge open meta-narratives with value, hope, virtue, dilemma, heroism, tragedy, failure, redemption, resurrection, love, evil, justice. Human society which only sees and acknowledges its physical realities has little scope for development beyond the physicality of consumerism. This has become the dominant paradigm of post modernity. As an alternative, humanity more aware of its metaphysical nature, can engage with open meta-narratives inspired by myth to develop its spiritual life. Such a society and its constituent members will be far more concerned with its inner life than its outward possession or impression, with its qualities, its heart, its kindness, forgiveness, care, generosity, loves and loveliness than with its consumption pattern and its cool image. This is an outcome for which a synthesis of philosophy and religion would be worthwhile.

The detailed argument

The argument proceeds from a review of the contemporary understanding of humanity, through a critique of church, to a proposed model for a new synthesis. A brief review of the development of atheism and unbelief runs from Hume to Dawkins, includes other contemporary philosophers such as Simon Blackburn, Andre Comte-Sponville and Julian Baggini and the counter arguments of authors like Terry Eagleton, John Lennox and Antony Flew. The conclusion is that atheism is at least a viable strong hypothesis.

Other issues then discussed include the mixed and often disreputable history of religion, the greater impact of technology rather than of any God on humanity, and the major challenge of the Enlightenment to doctrinal religion. The Enlightenment is considered within a 'holistic history of humanity', showing the effect of its prioritising intellect, reason and logic and relegating emotion and spirituality. The interplay of choice, cause and chance is discussed as a refinement of the Enlightenment model.

Having reviewed the biological critique of God advanced by Dawkins and others, the case for theism from the observed order in the physical planetary world and the possible exogenous nature of mathematics and logic is examined.

The middle section of the book critiques contemporary church in its doctrinal, phenomenological and ritual forms, arguing against doctrinal interpretations and in favour of a strong myth interpretation to generate personal and social value meta-narratives.

This proposed synthesis of metaphysical philosophy and myth mediating religion is worked out in concept and in a range of examples in the final section of the book.

Humanity today

Why people don't believe

The atheist or agnostic argument is strong. There is no proof of God. People live their daily normal lives on the basis of encounters with demonstrable reality. They wake up to a physical world each morning and interact with that real demonstrable world. Of course this will include metaphysical feelings and emotions, hopes and loves, expectations and disappointments, ideas and uncertainties, but these themselves are located in real physical people and real experienced events. They are generated by and from real physical people and do not exist independently of them. No idea can exist without a person's brain to file it in. Demonstrable reality is essential to this way of life which would fail without it. If people only believed for example in a house, a transport network, their family and friends, without any exact corresponding physical reality of these things, then their life would crash. It would be unworkable. It would not be life as we know it. So it is not unreasonable to expect proof or demonstrability of all aspects of life. 'If you're in love, show me' says the song, and it's a reasonable request. So why should a God who it is claimed has invented this life which has a clear requirement of real time proven reality, then dodge this requirement himself and talk of faith and mystery as the way to comprehend and engage him? Reason as we shall see is important to human beings, and it is reasonable to expect anyone who wants to be taken seriously to be evident. God and faith in God cannot escape this existential urge.

Creation, complexity, Darwin and Dawkins

What evidence there is for God is equally good evidence for alternative atheist explanations. Creation is rightly thought to be amazing, but wrongly thought to prove the existence of a Creator. It is all too easy to point to the wonders of the creation, to

8

celebrate its creative genius, to wonder at its sunsets, to rejoice at the cuddly winsome newborn baby animal of any species. These things are beauty and joy. But when they are set against the hostility of the climate and the sheer destruction of one species by another in the hierarchy of the food chain, then this beauty is quickly compromised. Any creator has to account for the inbuilt destruction of the cosmos and not just take credit for its positive outcomes. This horrific destruction is not just a sideshow, some unfortunate by-product of creation, but is core and essential to its operation. Sunsets inspire awe and poetry, but tsunamis kill hundreds of thousands at a stroke. The endearing lion cub will one day ferociously and painfully tear the flesh of its live prey. In a restaurant close to where I live there is an endearing framed photograph of a tiger and its cub with the words 'My God will supply all your need' written alongside it. There is no photograph of a gazelle or zebra with any similar Bible quotation.

A more powerful argument for the existence of God is that, regardless of the moral mixture of the climate and the animal world, its very complexity requires a designer. The apologetic set out by William Paley in his 'Natural Theology' argued from a watch whose existence needed a designer, that complexity does need design and therefore that there is a God. The Scottish philosopher David Hume had already contested this 'watch-maker' argument in the eighteenth century, principally because it fails to take account of the dysfunctionality of the creation. Snowflakes are also unique and complex but are generated without conscious design. Our concept of what is complex is in any case subjective and relative. And if explanation of the natural world required a designer, that is far less than a concept of God, and would in turn need explanation. Hume's contemporary, Diderot, similarly rejected the argument. Nevertheless this consideration of the wonder and complexity of creation, for example the delicate complex instrument of the eye, has played an important role in suggesting the existence of a creator God or at least of an intelligent designer. It is this core point which has been freshly challenged and found wanting by current neo-Darwinian writers.

In his earlier work, 'The Selfish Gene' and 'The Blind Watchmaker', the latter so entitled to counteract Paley's apologetic, the renowned zoologist Richard Dawkins developed a credible neo-Darwinian hypothesis that complexity does not need design. The eye can evolve randomly through millennia from light sensitive skin in earlier species giving them survival advantage which then leads to a chain random process of the same logic to eventually generate the complex eye. No designer is needed. This is a valid hypothesis, but it does rest on the Darwinian assumptions of prolific random mutations including improved capability mutations, and a hostile selective climate. In some ways Darwin's theory was not sufficiently random. Once stochastic probability functions are introduced into the scheme, the result may be the survival of the luckiest rather than the survival of the fittest. And if hostile constraints are relaxed or removed we may see the survival of everything and everyone, not just the fittest or the luckiest. Certainly as technology has reined in the hostility of the climate and sheltered humanity from its worst attacks, the world population has grown immensely. As one wag once joked, the greatest empirical challenge to the concept of the survival of the fittest is his own survival. Perhaps many of us ruefully agree.

So some aspects of Darwin's theory of evolution may need to evolve further themselves. The concept of competitive proliferation is represented in human reproduction where literally millions of male sperm compete to fertilise each single female egg. But the theory does have a major problem in being defined over millennia so that its processes cannot be recreated for observation in real time and its data points are rare. It is not clear for example what process is proposed for the development of the long neck in a giraffe. Did proliferation generate multiple species of giraffe-like animals with varying neck length whilst the vegetation either all migrated higher or was entirely consumed at lower levels by the shorter neck animals? How come the vegetation height increased exactly in time for the millennia required for a species to evolve a longer neck? Giraffes in any case commonly eat lower vegetation. The evolutionist's current answer to this is that the giraffe initially evolved long legs to run fast to escape its predators and then found it needed to evolve a long neck to drink. This shows how inventive the theory can be. If humans evolved from apes, how come only the ape and human species survived and not all the intermediary species? And looking into the future is it credible that humans will evolve for example flight if this proves to be of competitive advantage, which it probably is? Critique of Darwin's theory does not at all have to imply deism. Whatever the exact specification of Darwinian theory it is still a powerful hypothesis that some such mechanistic process led to the present outcome of species, including human beings, and that no God is necessary to have achieved this complex amazing and wondrous result.

Dawkins' early work is attractively written, richly informed from his extensive academic knowledge of zoology, and convincing of his main hypothesis. Debate continues over whether natural selection operates at the level of the gene as Dawkins proposes, or at the level of the seed, the organism, some specific trait, the individual animal, or the whole species, and whether competition is between or within species. Mathematical models try to show that sexual selection and foraging are optimised. Altruism, especially between strangers meeting once only, remains difficult to explain. Nevertheless, complexity in biology is possible without design and does not necessarily imply design and therefore the existence of a designer. Even though a designer is far less than religious definitions of God, the designer argument cannot be used to suggest God or some sub-set of God as designer. However, as we shall see later, Dawkins' establishment of a random undesigned route to biological complexity does not apply to explain the order in the physical world of the planets and their complex mathematical order, or the apparently exogenous nature of mathematical logic itself.

Less convincing also, or simply scientifically incorrect methodology, is his leap to conclude that he has therefore eliminated alternative hypotheses. Complexity according to Dawkins' hypothesis does not need design. However the alternative hypothesis remains valid. Complexity can still imply design, although *not necessarily* and it is this last qualifying point that Dawkins has introduced. Karl Popper's scientific methodology is set out in his 'The Logic of Scientific Discovery'. Popper defines the scientific process as one of observing data and phenomena and then constructing explanatory hypotheses. These hypotheses never attain the status of absolute truth but have to be content to remain hypotheses. Doubt is essential to the intellectual scientific process. Moreover, to be valid, hypotheses have to be falsifiable by having testable empirical implications. Generating logical implications from hypotheses and testing these implications empirically leads to the rejection, refining and/or retention of the hypothesis which therefore itself evolves through the process. Good hypotheses prove durable, resilient to the implication and verification process, but even they never become absolute truth. Popper's criterion of falsifiability is not easily applied to theories of history, whether Darwinian or Marxist, or to theories of probability, neither of which can be readily replicated.

However we can say on this basis that it's not *true* that complexity does or that it doesn't need design. Both are valid hypotheses

which need to be continually tested against their empirical implications. It's easy to show that complexity can result from design
and Dawkins has shown that it can result without design too.
But that's all he has shown.

Even less convincing therefore is the way Dawkins has subsequently launched an unremitting campaign against religion.
Unfortunately he has become a campaigner rather than a thinker.
His later very popular book 'The God Delusion' is a diatribe
claiming to disprove God because there is no proof of God, and
because of extreme practices by weird church groups often in the
United States who dramatically and in some cases obscenely
denounce homosexuality, along with other groups who demonstrate well known detestable religious bigotry etc. The Old
Testament material of the Bible with its morally deficient
Yahweh is great grist to Dawkins' mill. Dawkins has then set up
a web site on which he offers to deliver people from religion,
becoming himself some sort of messianic deliverance figure. All
this is unhelpful to his original powerful and intellectual contribution of the hypothesis of biological complexity without design.
Nevertheless he has become the established high priest of neo-
Darwinian atheism.

We now review theistic responses from writers like Terry
Eagleton, Antony Flew and John Lennox and more subtle
arguments for atheism from Simon Blackburn, Andre Comte-
Sponville and Julian Baggini.

Contemporary philosophers

A recent strong academic critique of Dawkins is offered by Terry
Eagleton in his 'Reason, Faith and Revolution'. Eagleton is a
surprising combination of former Catholic believer and Marxist.
He derides much of what Dawkins and Christopher Hitchens

author of 'God is not Great' write, somewhat disrespectfully labelling them as 'Ditchkins'. He is contemptuous of their Oxford/Washington/neocon scene, adding in Martin Amis, Salman Rushdie and Ian McEwan for good measure. His main critique is that whilst Dawkins and Hitchens critique religion, they do not apply the same critique to science or the enlightened modernity they promote, summed up in their castigation of the Inquisition but not of Hiroshima, although he makes this extraordinary suggestion that Dawkins and Hitchens do not object to Hiroshima without asking them. Eagleton however commits the same errors he accuses Dawkins and Hitchens of. They, says Eagleton, attack a straw man of extremist religion rather than its more credible expressions and interpretations – 'this straw targeting of Christianity is now drearily commonplace' he complains - whilst Eagleton himself attacks Dawkins and Hitchens rather than the more credible atheist arguments of Simon Blackburn, Andre Comte-Sponville, Julian Baggini etc reviewed below. Eagleton simply assumes God. He is quickly writing in detail about the nature of God without any supporting argument – God is just as Eagleton says he is. He writes that he has given a theological account which he clearly hasn't. He has simply speculated on some ideal fabrication of an imagined God. And Jesus is Eagleton's revolutionary, a Che Guevara figure who stands for the poor, critiques the establishment, and himself suffers ignominy and bears injustice. This may be a worthy interpretation and one relevant to a synthesis proposed at the end of this book. Eagleton allows what he calls 'allegory' as an interpretative mechanism to those who cannot believe the Christian text as literally as he does. The key to the development of such allegory is the interpretative principle of myth which will be argued below as a strong rather than a weak interpretation of religion.

John Lennox's book 'God's Undertaker - Has Science Buried God?' is a very thoughtful, cogent, well informed and well written critique of the Dawkins hypothesis that complexity does not require design, perhaps the best of current critiques. He argues that the rationality and intelligibility of the universe supports a design hypothesis. The observation of irreducible complexity argues against random evolution from nothing. Micro adaptation of existing species cannot be extrapolated into macro evolution of new species. Mathematical algorithms of biological systems require an external information input and the Dawkins-Sober formulation also needs this external input and so fails to demonstrate a random blind process. This is all interesting, relevant and cogent, although Lennox frequently relies on great scientists for their views about God which in his own terms is a category error. Lennox may have established a hypothesis for a god of the first information bit, but this is a very far fling from the personal God of Christianity which he then leaps to in his last chapter on the basis of absolutely nothing. Given the careful interesting dissection of his argument to that point, this is a disappointing leap devoid of the same careful logic, and shows that Lennox started rather than concluded his thinking with a religious world view.

More thoughtful though less dramatic and high profile reasons for not believing in God are given by other contemporary thinkers including Simon Blackburn, Andre Comte-Sponville and Julian Baggini. Simon Blackburn, Professor of Philosophy at Cambridge University, in chapter 5 of his readable introduction to philosophy 'Think', carefully dissects the known set of arguments for the existence of God and shows that none are credible. Andre Comte-Sponville, Professor of Philosophy at the Sorbonne in Paris does the same in chapter 7 of his 'The Little Book of Philosophy' and then proceeds in chapter 8 to set out reasons for atheism. He finds any idea of God as father unacceptable on the grounds that a good father would not be absent from his children, sending them only indirect messages.

Comte-Sponville often visits a large Paris children's hospital and cannot accept a God who 'abandons gazelles to tigers and children to cancer'. He finds humanity too faulted to be explained by divine creation.

In his more recent book 'The Book of Atheist Spirituality' Comte-Sponville summarises his arguments against the existence of God. Like most philosophers he finds Saint Anselm's ontological 'a priori' proof that by definition some perfect ultimate being exists unconvincing. The same for Leibniz's cosmological proof that the universe is contingent (ie it could also not have been) and therefore there is an ultimate reason. The 'physico-theological' proof or the 'intelligent design' or 'watchmaker' proof is inadequate because as David Hume pointed out it fails to explain the dysfunctionality in the universe. Furthermore if God exists he should be more evident. Evil is too enormous and humanity too mediocre. Common ideas of God are too close to a likely fantasy.

Julian Baggini in 'What's It All About? Philosophy and the Meaning of Life' makes similar points. John Humphrys in his 'In God We Doubt' records radio interviews he conducted with Rowan Williams, Archbishop of Canterbury for the Christian faith, Jonathan Sacks Chief Rabbi in the UK for the Jewish faith and Tariq Ramadan, a Moslem academic, for Islam. None of these three leaders of mainstream religion were able to adequately answer Humphrys' questioning of the existence of God and specifically of the suffering of innocent children. Constantly Humphrys is unconvinced by their attempts to answer and persuade. In similar vein Robert Tressel in his great socialist novel 'The Ragged Trousered Philanthropists' criticises not only capitalism but also religion with his example of an emaciated starving cat whose struggle for survival proves that if there is a God, he cannot be all-knowing, all-caring and all-powerful and is therefore not much of a God.

The weight of contemporary philosophy is therefore towards the atheist or agnostic conclusion with unconvincing attempts by Eagleton, Flew and Lennox to offer a theistic view. This conclusion from a priori thinking finds further support in the historical reality of religion.

The history of religion

The historic record of religion and Christianity in particular is also negative. Diarmaid MacCulloch in his great chronicle 'Reformation – Europe's House Divided' describes the unbelievable judicial burning alive by Protestant and Catholic governments of priests and laity believing or practising differently. 300 people died in four years of Queen Mary's Catholic England. French Huguenots had their tongues cut out before being burned. Anabaptists were drowned in the river Limmat. Calvin agreed to Servetus' execution in Geneva and made no objection to his being burned alive. Tyndale was offered the 'mercy' of being hung rather than burned for his work in producing an English Bible. This is all a dreadful record of schism which continues today in milder form. The church continually fragments into smaller units which are defined more by what they are against rather than what they are in favour of. Protestants are so called because of their protest against the established church and its practices. As Bishop Richard Holloway discovered at the Anglican church's Lambeth conference in 1998, it is not only the content of entrenched positions, in this case on homosexuality, which is disappointing and offensive, but more the venom with which anyone holding other views is attacked. Grace is quickly dropped where belligerents have their minutely defined attachment to their specific truth. Often those with theologies claiming to be based on grace show least of it. Islam too has its share of atrocities, for example in the infamous massacre of several hundred Banu

Qurayza Jews by Muhammed in Medina in 627AD. The 1947 partition of India displaced 14 million people leading to atrocious violence between Hindu and Moslem communities with the massacre of around 500,000. Even in 1992 Hindu groups destroyed the only mosque in Ayodhya leading to widespread Hindu/Moslem violence throughout India. Religion has rarely been pacific.

Technology is god ?

In the meantime technology advanced as faith receded. Technology is the reconfiguration and deliberate engineering of natural processes discovered by scientific research. It connects humanity to its context of the universe and is the only thing standing between them. It is partly a freely given endowment to humanity in that the natural processes pre-exist, and partly value added by humanity's effort, first in isolating the process, and then in harnessing it in a different configuration of processes. It has, as hinted in our introduction, become more determinant of the human situation than any God. Without contraceptive technology many more human beings would have been born. Many more are being born with fertility technology. Without advancing medical technology many more would have died.

Technology has therefore fundamentally altered the balance of the human population and its life expectancy. It has also drastically altered its quality of life. By taming and harnessing the elements, technology has shifted humanity from being subject to the cosmos and powerless before it to being relatively more its master. The shift is not total but it is substantial. Protection against wind, rain and sun is available, although earthquakes and tsunamis remain overwhelming. Health is vastly improved. Diseases like smallpox have been totally eradicated and there is technology in place to control other potential epidemics. At the same time, stress related diseases have increased and the AIDS virus remains elusive as does the common cold. Nevertheless health outcomes are undeniably better. Vastly fewer women die in childbirth and infants in childhood. Pain where it occurs is better controlled and mitigated, whether in dentistry or in end of life cancer suffering. Some types of cancers themselves are being overcome. Gout is controlled and no longer leads to amputation. Antibiotics have greatly reduced bacterial infections.

Technology has also altered the production function, so that the number of person hours required to produce anything and therefore to achieve any given standard of living has fallen immensely, and in consequence the amount of product from a growing population has soared, leading to the rampant consumer age. It has thus also released time for people to develop arts and other interests beyond the requirements of mere survival. So life itself, the length of life, the quality of life and lifestyle are all heavily determined by technology. God who claims creation and fatherhood of humanity has made no such advances available but has stayed remarkably silent. His silence during major sufferings, for example of bubonic plague, and the silence of his book on the subject is a major indictment. Progress has been entirely a result of socially networked human effort.

This technology can however threaten to become a god itself, determining the future of humanity which created it. The servant can become the master. The German philosopher Martin Heidegger coined the phrase 'only a god can save us' and many applied this to the perceived threat of mega technologies such as nuclear technology with its ability to destroy the entire world. Rachel Carson's 'Silent Spring' aroused awareness of the threats of fertiliser and pesticide technology. The effect of carbon emitting technology on the environment and the threat of global warming has become the latest mega concern. It seemed that the 'thing', the artefact of technology, was now a process out of control.

There is clearly a possible danger of such technology control in that societal processes, as Aristotle, Durkheim, Hegel and others have pointed out, can become reified, a totality greater than the sum of the parts, and thus grow beyond control. Research laboratories around the world, greatly enabled by Internet sharing of developments in the scientific community, are bound to go where the science leads. Technology is essentially morally neutral. It is entirely amoral. A knife can be used to prepare a meal but also to kill an enemy. Nuclear technology can produce electricity without carbon emissions but it can also eradicate mass numbers of people in a bomb. So far the prophets of doom have been wrong in fearing a mega techno initiated catastrophe, and as a result they have failed to draw sufficient attention to the more subtle ways in which technological progress is shifting humanity.

There is a need for moral control of the technology beast so that it remains servant and not master, but on the other hand technology will evolve in an unstoppable way. If one government bans stem cell research then another will allow it. Morality is not sufficiently independent of technology. C Wright Mills' phrase that 'might is right' is too often too true. It is the powerful nations of the world that say what is OK and what is not, what is legislated and legitimate. Currently the United States has overwhelming military technology power. It can bomb and has bombed its way, for example into Iraq. It has armed the state of Israel with superior power to its neighbours so that it is able to dictate terms in Lebanon and Gaza. China has subjugated Tibet. One can only wonder what the outcome would be if some other power than the US happened to have the upper hand with overwhelming military technology. The US used nuclear bomb technology against the Japanese cities of

Hiroshima and Nagasaki in August 1945 with devastating effect. There would have been an immense difference in outcome for the world if Hitler's Nazi regime had developed this technology only a few years earlier. We assume that might and right co-exist, or we hope that they do. But the possibility that they might not, or the opinion that they currently do not, argue for greater power to be ascribed to equal voice institutions such as the United Nations.

European intellectual cynicism, American believerism and Asian religion

So, there is sufficient reason for unbelief and insufficient reason for belief. This position appears to be the one expressed by the large majority of Europeans who rarely if ever go to church, express any belief in God, read any religious text, or involve themselves in any religious practice other than the rites of passage. The Cartesian revolution insisted on the need and the right to doubt in its pursuit of the intellectual, philosophical and scientific quest. Doubt remains essential to the intellectual process and has inevitably transferred into religion, questioning and often dislodging belief. Two world wars and their millions dead devastated naive hopes in any triumphant good and even though illogically, since these were human disasters, also in God who failed to save even his so called chosen people from holocaust. They walked into the valley of the shadow of death and evil consumed them.

Whilst separation of church and state is fundamental to the American Constitution, in Europe it is the separation of church and culture which has become almost total, apart from the momentary rites of passage of birth, marriage and death for the minority who recognise these in a church context.

21

This raises the question as to why religious belief remains strong in the United States and is resurgent in many parts of Asia whilst it has declined so markedly in Europe. The answer to this asymmetry lies in the cultural distinctives. Europe birthed the Enlightenment with its quintessential intellectual doubt and questioning. It also suffered the misery of continent-wide war, death and misery. Both of these led to an intellectual maturity and a prevalent cynicism. The contrast in America is the survival of naive hope which powers the society and gives it its strength. Where Europeans are cynical, Americans are believing. The excess of this naivety is humorously sent up in Mark Twain's Huckleberry Finn where the duke and the king effortlessly con successive communities along the Mississippi from their travelling raft. It is endlessly exploited by commercial religion, one example being T L Osborne in Tulsa Oklahoma who climbed to the top of his university prayer tower and determined to stay there until either God took him, or his supporters contributed the funds he needed at the time. Needless to say the latter lesser miracle was the one that happened, although the former may have had more effect on cynical unbelievers. Similar exploitation can be viewed every day with regular monotony on US television channels where religious speakers invite donations whilst counters rocket up towards their multimillion $ targets.

This somewhat naive belief has its advantages. Cynicism can become an all too easy and lazy route. It can be entertaining, but inevitably has comparatively negative outcomes. Entrepreneurs who fail in UK society are derided, whereas in US society they are encouraged to have another go. Airport taxi drivers in the USA can describe wonderfully hopeful plans, strategies and expectations for the expansion of their business whilst their European counterparts sink in well practised and sophisticated complaint. Partly this has to do with the existence of more historic institutions in European culture. These enable but also constrain people, and certainly attract their blame for whatever happens or fails to happen in life. American culture is more recent and has therefore developed less dependence on institutions and placed more expectation on the individual. The combination of this different intellectual climate, more believing than doubting or cynical, together with the acceptance and even worship of commercial success, accounts for church attendance and growth in the USA. US pastors are often not averse to calling their church activities 'businesses'. The standard US church is very formulistic and is characterised by unchallenged belief statements, a happy club mentality, and the same splurge of a sea of cash which is available to other American clubs such as their classical orchestras.

Asian cultures are more historic and more complex to analyse in terms of their interaction with religious belief. Confucian religion was suppressed in China by Mao's communist regime but not eradicated in the roots of the culture. Christianity, although similarly suppressed, is growing rapidly in modern China. Shintoism and Taoism remain strong in Japan. Asian societies appear to be more conformist than European society and therefore beliefs are less questioned. The Enlightenment did not happen in Asia. Rather Enlightenment thinking filtered into Asian culture whose pragmatism applied it where it was useful, for example in industry and medicine, without allowing it to challenge the core social paradigm and its religion. Deference to the institutions of society, including its religion, is high in Asian cultures and low to non existent in European society.

And yet religious practice in Japan is less an intellectual conviction than a valued component of a more holistic understanding of life. In this context religion does not then compete with intellectualisation and is relatively immune from its onslaught. It is possible to practise such religion without necessarily consciously and cognitively believing any creed. Ethical foundations may also be different. For example Singapore practised a mild form of genetic engineering by financial incentive where Chinese ethnic graduate parents received substantial funding for a third child which were not available to parents of other ethnic groups or to less educated parents. On being challenged about this practice a leading churchman commented to me that our western ethics were irrelevant. Whatever view one takes of this and other issues, it certainly suggests that different ethical foundations characterise different world cultures, altering the balance of principle and pragmatism. Values are variable in different social and religious contexts.

In summary, we have so far seen why people largely don't believe, through lack of demonstrable evidence, because evolution has displaced creation, because of defective moral aspects of religious faith and a religious God, because of technology's superior determining effect on human life, because of the success of Enlightenment reason and logic. How has humanity then developed? The next section offers a view of this as a process of change in the holistic emphasis through human history.

A Holistic History of Humanity

There is no doubt that humanity has gone through a paradigm shift in the last few hundred years. The shift from a rural agricultural society to an urban industrial society has had huge consequences. Physically people live longer, are healthier and taller. Life offers a bigger agenda. There are more possibilities. But there is less community, more anonymity and consequently more loneliness.

Compared to the very long timescales of several millennia required for evolution of a species in the Darwinian account, the human species has undergone immense change in a far shorter period of a few thousand years, and has experienced an even greater pace of change in the last few hundred years. The context for humanity is changing far more rapidly than any mutation of its species can possibly adapt to. Photographs of only 100 years ago show people living in a very different context from today's. If we had similar photographs of 500 years ago, 1,000 years ago and 10,000 years ago, the difference would be stunning. Anthropologists, with the help of archaeologists, are able to infer much about the life of earlier civilisations. Some of them were advanced. For example it is claimed that in the year 910 AD Arab civilisation was so advanced that it was possible to cash a cheque in Barcelona drawn from a bank account in Baghdad. Felipe Fernandez Armesto gives this and many other examples of early advanced civilizations in his 'Millennium : A History of our last Thousand Years'. Theodore Zeldin paints a similar picture of refined life in the eleventh century Japanese court in his 'An Intimate History of Humanity'. Humans developed from cave and forest dwellers and from hunters to farmers, eventually forming and populating cities. Technology and the associated organisation of production enabled and drove each step of change.

The context of human life has clearly changed immensely, but has the human being changed to the same extent? It is difficult to imagine how people were, how they lived and worked, thought and loved, knew joy and pain at these various stages of change. Did cavemen sing, recite poetry, tell jokes? Was love tender, or was the climate and context so hostile that the struggle to survive exhausted all human resource and left no energy for wider expression? We are very aware of the holistic nature of human beings today, but is emotional and spiritual expression a luxury?

Did physicalism reign supreme to the extent that metaphysics was irrelevant? Certainly knowledge was more limited. People knew less. Fewer facts, less intellectualisation, fewer ideas. Perhaps they wondered more and had other more highly developed senses?

We can trace a holistic history of humanity more accurately over the last 2,000 years since we have access to written records. Over this period we can see how human civilisation, and therefore what it meant to be a human, being changed its emphasis between physical, intellectual, spiritual and emotional definitions. It is fascinating to see how the veneration of intellect of Greek philosophy, with implied and often explicit disdain for body and emotion, gave way to dominance of the more limited physical concept of man in Europe's dark ages, until the Enlightenment rediscovered the intellectual pursuit and became Platonic, with the same unease of the body and emotion characteristic of Platonism. Later this Enlightenment itself gave way to the emotional focus of Romanticism and modernity morphed into post modernity.

Of the civilisations of antiquity, Greece elevated the philosophical intellectualisation of Socrates, Plato, Aristotle, Ptolemy, Pythagoras. Philosophy or 'the love of wisdom' was born in this era and the long conversational debates between Greek philosophers are read and studied avidly today, although to the modern ear they are somewhat drawn out and rather pompous. Plato's 'Republic' written in about 380 BC in this Socratic dialogue style, separates the human soul into three elements of mind, spirit and body and then devises a city state with a structure to match these elements ruled by philosopher kings with guardians, auxiliaries, and working classes to operate it. In the dialogue Socrates discusses justice at length, questioning whether a just person thought to be unjust is happier or not than an unjust person thought to be just – ie whether the essence of justice is more valuable than its appearance and consequent social acceptance. He discusses community, marriage, limits to war, and philosophical education. The city state is ruled by a philosopher elite which he sees as degenerating into oligarchy, democracy and tyranny. His allegory of the cave shows how and why he considers the philosopher a superior leader of society, and why he considers philosophy essential to just leadership of society. His thinking is the main source of inspiration for his pupil Aristotle's 'Politics' and for the Christian Saint Augustine's 'The City of God'. Karl Popper in his 1945 'The Open Society and its Enemies' critiques Plato's city state as totalitarian. Whatever its merits or defects, the Republic is a clear demonstration of an intellectually aware society, and indeed of a society that regarded intellect as the supreme ruling characteristic of humanity and of human society.

Plato's division of the human persona into mind, body and spirit lives on today. His prioritisation of the mind became reflected deeply in twentieth century western society which shared his disdain for emotion and body. Men don't cry, the British upper lip is stiff, and sex is a huge neurosis of guilt and distortion. His championing of intellectual superiority, and therefore of the rule of the philosopher, was later incarnated in the Enlightenment. The philosophical education he recommended became core in the French educational system, though sadly absent from standard British education to its clear loss. What Plato did not achieve was a statement of or a vision for holistic humanity. He saw mind, body and spirit as separable, with intellect as superior, emotion less worthy, and body as the low order of the person. This value rating contradicts a holistic view and therefore does not help to understand and enable holistically integrated humanity.

Mind, emotion and body interact closely in the whole human persona, but framing their interaction ideally has proved very elusive throughout human history. Instead society has swung unhelpfully from one partial emphasis to another, with either physical bodily needs, urges and actions, or intellectual thought and rationality, or the emotional feel factor dominating. Nevertheless in his triumphing of the intellect, Plato established an intellectual tradition which was then lost. It remained buried and apparently dead until revived by the early writers of the Renaissance exemplified by Michel de Montaigne in the second half of the sixteenth century AD, ie some 1600 years later, and was only later in 1637 enunciated in Descartes famous phrase 'I think therefore I am'.

Contrary to the Greek empire, its successor Rome emphasised military might and physical indulgence, its bread and circuses leading eventually to its decline and defeat, according to Gibbons' thesis. Rome was hedonistic and cruel and in this sense brutal and crude. Its occupation of Judea left thousands of Jews crucified and the city eventually sacked. In this dichotomy we already see an early example of the failure of human society to achieve a holistic synthesis, to regard the physical and the intellectual as fully interactive, as mutually dependent, as what it is to be fully human. Barbarian hordes representing an even more physical humanity then broke the thread between antiquity and modernity, enforcing a long period of dark and middle ages, when the light seemed to have gone out, when physical animal predominated over intellectual human.

Enlightened humanity

Hence the triumph of the Enlightenment, restoring and valuing intellect, spirit and mind, and displacing feudal power with logic's rule. Indeed the challenge for post modernity's rejection of the rule of logic is the very real threat of the return of crude feudalism as the main competing power system. The Enlightenment's primacy of the mind and spirit linked back to Plato, but often carried with it embarrassment of the body which was seen as crude, leading to a non tactile world and to huge continuing western neurosis over sex. The pendulum again swung to the opposite extreme – acclaiming the intellectual human and denying the physical animal.

The Enlightenment, the Age of Reason, Modernity, triumphed extensively and changed humanity's life experience and life context, if not changing humanity itself. Certainly it changed humanity's awareness of itself. Understanding the reason and cause in the universe allowed science to drive technology to massively extend humanity's control and capability, hugely increase its productivity, and construct a whole new life experience. As with reason in the world of science and technology, so reasonableness became the criterion in matters of morality, of law, of human treatment. Inevitably as with all social focuses, the reaction came in the Romantic movement, which hailed free expression of emotions and feelings which had no necessary logic. An even stronger reaction occurred in the formation of Post Modernity whose philosophers, led by Foucault, objected to this very rule of logic, felt over-constrained by it, and demanded freedom even against logic for humanity.

The great process of change of the Enlightenment had its roots in the sixteenth century Renaissance, its first expression in the seventeenth century, and its great outpourings in the eighteenth century. It broke down the previous world views in cosmology, anthropology and theology inherited from Greek philosophy. The intellectual revolution of the Enlightenment led to the industrial revolution of the nineteenth and twentieth centuries which further developed and implemented the Enlightenment. Only later was the Enlightenment challenged in post modernity.

The Enlightenment was preceded by the sixteenth century Copernican revolution in which Copernicus (1473-1543), Galileo (1564-1642) and Kepler (1571-1630) established the heliocentric configuration and orbits of the planets around the sun. The early Renaissance then released the creative role of the person, which the Enlightenment took further by specifying the human mind as the sole source of meaning and value. Max Weber described modernity as the loss of an unquestioned legitimacy of a divinely instituted order. The process is essentially away from an *exogenous* causal purposeful view of human existence towards an *endogenous* view where existence, cause and purpose are all generated from within rather than sourced without in an external God. Reason or rationality, and not God, is the ultimate authority in the Enlightenment scheme.

The timeline of various contributors to the great intellectual awakening is set out on the following page.

As the table shows, thinking was wide and varied but did converge to a set of essential core concepts of

- an **anthropocentric** world view – humanity is central
- **physicalism** – only matter exists and all human functions are physical
- **endogenous metaphysics** – humanity generates its own metaphysics – none are exogenous
- **human consciousness** is the sole existential reality
- **reason** is the prime aspect and sole authority within human consciousness and the external world
- **reasonableness** directs ethical judgments, leading to liberal politics and economics

The Enlightenment is therefore hugely radical and has major implications, but yet is only heuristic. It is a methodology. It posits principles. But it has no content, a point which was central to Vico and Hegel's later critiques. There is no agenda, only a way of developing one. It is not holistic in emphasising intellectual reasoning above physical pleasure and emotion. It can suggest a negation of all prior human experience, development and institution. As in Plato's Republic it is elitist in implying higher value to intellectual capacity, as Voltaire for example clearly did. It is inconsistent in insisting that human consciousness is the prime existential reality, but in then identifying reason as the prime authority for that consciousness, whilst showing that reason also determines the external world and is derived from it. Its concepts of cause and choice are also inconsistent.

Its contributors were by no means fully enlightened. Francis Bacon endorsed torture. Descartes considered that animals felt no pain and therefore endorsed and practised vivisection. Newton wrote more about religion than he did about science. In his role at the Royal Mint he hounded counterfeiters including William Chaloner whose conviction and sentence to a cruel slow hanging, in fact a semi humane limitation of the exact sentence of hanging, drawing and quartering, Newton obtained after a farcically short trial, rather like Inspector Javert's hounding of Jean Valjean in Hugo's 'Les Miserables'. He probably died from mercury poisoning resulting from his pursuit of the divine spark in alchemy. Voltaire believed in God and in enlightened monarchy, distrusting democracy. Many retained a religious faith which may have been a reasoned conviction, or due to the full implications of Enlightenment thought not being worked through, or to the simple fear of persecution – it was after all only in 1697 that the 21 year old student Thomas Aikenhead was hanged in Edinburgh for criticising Christianity. There is also a healthy diversity of thought amongst Enlightenment philosophers. Descartes, Locke, Newton, Vico, Voltaire and Rousseau were deists, Spinoza, Hume, Diderot, La Mettrie and d'Holbach were not. Kant and Voltaire celebrated reason, whilst Vico, Hume and Rousseau held emotions and myth as equally or more important. But this underlines the quintessential nature of the Enlightenment – it was not a new replacement creed – it was methodology and not content – you could believe what you wanted as long as you reasoned it and did not impose it.

Enlightenment time line

	17th century	18th century	main themes
Rene Descartes	1596-1650		self consciousness is the defining point of and for humanity body/mind dualism, so endorsed animal vivisection nominalism leaves space for God also developed Cartesian mathematics, algebra and geometry
Baruch Spinoza	1632-1677		single body/mind substance has endogenous power pantheist and determinist
John Locke	1632-1704		political and economic liberalism, mind is formed by education considered Christianity 'reasonable'
Isaac Newton	1643-1727		motion does not require a divine first mover mechanism in absolute time and space mathematics of gravitational attraction developed the mathematical calculus, optics and alchemy hostile disputes with Leibniz, Hooke, Flamsteed wrote extensively on religion and Bible prosecuted counterfeiters – William Chaloner was cruelly hung
Gottfried Leibniz	1646-1716		virtual 'mondas' exist with endogenous purpose and action ie not only Newtonian atoms with mechanistic movement rather like 'selfish genes'?
Giambattista Vico	1668-1744		also developed the mathematical calculus myth, cyclical history and Providence are as important as reason
Voltaire		1694-1778	a deist but religion must be subordinated to reason
David Hume		1711-1776	there is no separate soul, reason subject to emotion and will rejected the designer argument for creation
Denis Diderot		1713-1784	the universe does not require a divine designer
Jean-Jacques Rousseau		1712-1778	hypothesised evolution of species by natural selection also a deist but emphasised the primacy of freedom feelings more important than reason, promotes democracy
Julian Offray de La Mettrie		1709-1751	total physicalism - refuting Descartes body/mind dualism 'the soul is only …. a physical part of the brain' animals have senses, humans just more
Baron d'Holbach		1723-1789	total physicalism
Immanuel Kant		1724-1804	emancipation of mankind through an unconditional acceptance of the authority of reason space and time relative to human perception also demonstrated tidal friction drag retarding global spin
Georg Hegel		1774-1831	many and varied but developed Aristotle's concept of totality

Cogito Ergo Sum

This is Descartes famous phrase 'I think therefore I am'. It has been taken out of context but nevertheless used as pithy shorthand for the Enlightenment celebration of reason and logic which require a capacity to think. Humanity and human existence is cognitive, has consciousness, is self aware. As a partial truth this is great revelation and liberation. Free thinking is creative. It challenges institutions, traditions and personal preconceptions. It can discover new facts, new truths, new interpretations. It can devise new hypotheses and test them. It can generate great art. It can reform corrupt practice. It can produce wonderful humour. It can extend self potential. But it is not a total definition and in this sense the short phrase is a lie. Not only do we think, but we also feel. Our emotions are not subject to rationality. Appreciation of art, of a sunset, of a friend or a lover is more than and different to rational thought. And thought has its limits. As Jesus said 'which of you by taking thought can add one cubit to his stature?'. People with limited thinking ability are still fully people. At its worst it is totally platonic and denies the physical and emotional elements of the holistic human, leading to all the suppression of body and emotion we have discussed.

It also conflates the concept of reason and reasonable, both of which were important to the Enlightenment although they were often not clearly distinguished. Reason applies to mathematics, to science, to logic. Reasonable applies to behaviour, to law and to human interaction. One tends to the absolute, the other is definitely relative. Reason may correctly link cause and effect and be used for prediction. Reasonable is entirely more subtle a concept. Take a criminal case like the theft of bread by Jean Valjean in Victor Hugo's 'Les Miserables'. We quickly understand the reason for the theft – his family is poor and starving. But the question of what is reasonable justice is the larger issue Hugo pursues in the novel.

Enlightened ethics will be less quick to condemn, and there is a connection with reason here because understanding the reason for someone's act leads to more reasonable treatment of the act. Nevertheless, whilst the reason may be unique, the definition of what is reasonable is not, and a wide range of opinion is possible. The Enlightenment was an enlightenment of values as well as of logic. Torture was eschewed as a legal mechanism. Again there is logic in this in that a tortured person may well say anything to avoid pain, and there is no guarantee that truth is extracted. But the opposition was on the grounds of moral enlightenment too. Capital punishment was also removed from the law - with the logic that it is irreversible in the case of a later proven miscarriage of justice, but with moral approbation of judicial killing per se as well. Enlightenment ethics were redefined according to what was reasonable, rather than what was decreed by a former feudal ethic. In some cases this led to libertarian views - anything goes. And why not? At least some rational reason had to be given for an ethical code to make it reasonable.

Choice, Cause and Chance

The Enlightenment Age of Reason showed the importance of causal relationship in its explanation of phenomena. Words like 'because' (thinking backwards) and 'therefore' (thinking forwards) worked this causal paradigm. Once a causal mechanism in science had been established then it could be reconfigured, harnessed by technology, and implemented in a wide set of applications. The causal link between magnetic field rotation and electric current, between bacteria and illnesses, between evaporation and cooling were all researched and re-engineered. Everything had a reason. Human behaviour could also be explained by its causes, whether these were physiological, neurological or from exogenous cause, and human relationships were seen to be the result of causal phenomena.

At the same time, the enlightened human being was seen to be a cognitive being and to have freedom of choice. The mantra of choice is strong in private consumer markets and in public sector policymaking today. We can choose our lifestyle, the goods and services we consume, down to their detailed specification. The days of Henry Ford's offer of any colour as long as it was black have gone. At more philosophical levels, cognitive aware humanity can decide its economic outcomes and does not have to be pushed around by some dumb 'market'. It can determine its work/life mix, the degree of harmony in its interaction with the ecology – it can, as the ancient Bible text suggested, rule the earth and subdue it.

It is fascinating that these two great concepts of the Enlightenment, cause and choice, are incompatible. If things are caused they are not chosen. This incompatibility has led to competing interpretations both in humanistic philosophy and in religion. The determinist school of philosophy sees the human being and all its actions as totally determined and outside any illusion of choice. This has important repercussions, for example in understanding criminal behaviour and society's appropriate response. Something that is not my choice is not my fault either. I am a deterministic machine. The alternative liberal school sees humanity as majestically exercising macro and micro choice, and it is this philosophy which is dominant and makes monarchs of us all. It makes potential entrepreneurs of us all too and sees our possibilities. It is therefore more inspiring as a world view. However it also makes demanding consumers of us.

In religion the divide between the deterministic and the free choice view has been ferocious, as is sadly often the case in matters of religious differences. The Calvinist school thought in terms of predestination. Since God is in authority it follows that he says what is to happen, sometimes to micro detail, but certainly to the point of personal salvation. This led to the contorted view in theology that only the elect previously determined by God would be saved. You did not choose me but I chose you said Jesus. All very depressing and demotivating. On the contrary the Arminian school believed in free choice for each individual to get it right or wrong, so that wrongdoing was a personal accountability, and each was free to accept God's offer of salvation or not, so that Christianity was a choice. Choose you this day whom you will serve said Joshua.

Of course choice brings potential and possibility but it also brings accountability and responsibility. In contemporary society it frustrates political leaders that people want the potential and the possibility without the accountability and the responsibility. At its best religion has a noble view of humanity in its view of humanity's creativity. God created the world and made man in his image. Creativity implies choice and action. It multiplies our potential and possibility but also our accountability and responsibility. Jesus told the parable of the talents in which different people were gifted differently but 'of him to whom much is given, much will be expected', ie that the talent should be used creatively according to its scope and potential.

So how much choice do we have in reality? Take this worn mantra of consumer choice. In reality if we could all choose the exact detail of everything we wanted, then a huge multiple of what we all consume would have to be manufactured and the bulk of it thrown away. Where are the non-chosen commodities? They don't exist, showing that we can only choose from what there is, and not from the universe of possibilities. Our choice is limited and even a 'made to order' concept doesn't give us total choice. This is even more the case where we come to public services. Politicians love to tell us that we can choose which school we or our children go to, which hospital and even which surgeon we are treated by, which train service operator we can travel with etc. Amazing! This is of course a myth in the weak sense of the word. Unless it works out that other parents exactly want the school I don't want, or other patients don't want the hospital and surgeon I want, or unless there is immense overprovision to allow this amazing choice, then the reality is that my choice is constrained. I can only choose from what there is.

Let's look at more fundamental questions of choice. Much of life is indeed chosen for us. We can't choose our birth and therefore our fundamental existence, or our parents, or our family. Even once born, many of our bodily functions are involuntary. We can't choose our heart beat – there is no switch or control and it is determined for us. We can choose not to breathe for a few moments but not for long without dire consequences. Our choices are constrained. As we grow out of nappies we can choose when we urinate or excrete but not whether we do. We have little or no control over how tall we grow.

The question of choice then moves up from basic physical phenomena to metaphysicals. Can I choose my mental capability? Can I choose my personality or my attitudes? Can I choose my behaviour or my values? And higher up the value chain can I choose my actions? And forward in life can I choose my friends, my partner, my career, my children?

It will be clear that in some cases there really is no choice. I cannot choose how clever I am or not, although I can choose how much to develop whatever level of intelligence I do have by my reading and educational decisions. I cannot choose my basic personality, but I can seek to manage my characteristics, cultivating the good aspects of love, generosity, forgiveness, and managing the negative tendencies to anger, impatience, hostility, unkindness, and the ubiquitous selfishness of the current age.

I will probably have very limited career choices, having to depend on what I am capable of, what education I end up following, what jobs are available. And friends and partners are not chosen from the universal set of possibilities. It depends on who I meet. I can choose not to befriend someone I meet, but I cannot choose to befriend someone I have not met or have only seen on television. Modern technology allows us to choose not to have children and is advancing its capability to allow us to choose to have children, but the choice is not total and the child we have may not follow our choices in who they are or how they live.

The degree of choice in behaviour is puzzling. How far am I programmed and how much can I choose? Can a kind person choose to be cruel? In which case can a cruel person choose to be kind? Kathleen Taylor in her recent book 'Cruelty – Human Evil and the Human Brain' defines cruelty as 'unjustified voluntary behaviour which causes foreseeable suffering to an undeserving victim' and then seeks to question how cruelty maps into neural patterns. A simpler definition may be that of 'doing something unnecessary to someone that they do not want', and therefore include a wide range of cruelties from unnecessarily denying a child an ice cream to the infamous brutal atrocities Taylor cites. On the core question as to how cruelty works through the human brain she comes to the disappointing conclusion that 'the brain sciences are not sufficient to understand it fully'. She explains cruel behaviour in terms of processes of 'otherization' and threat responses. She implies that analysis of the brain's neurons may

39

explain how cruelty is done, but she appears to retain the view
that the person is separate from these mechanisms and has choice
and responsibility for their actions, although she does not
expound this clearly. She suggests that, by engineering the
stimuli, we can reduce cruelty, but she does not address the
secular change in commonality of cruelty over time. Although
noting that public execution is now prohibited in developed
societies, she does not explain how utter social cruelties such as
the hanging, drawing and quartering of criminals can have arisen
in the first place and then rejected as unnatural and cruel. Who
thought of such horrors, and how did their minds think in this
sadistic way, who wrote them into the law, and who carried them
out?

Similarly can we choose to be generous or mean, or are we
already generous or mean as an unavoidable, inevitable
unchangeable attribute? It has been amply demonstrated by
experiment that peer group and other pressures can persuade
people to change their actions and for example to torture
someone. The Nazi regime turned very ordinary, apparently
worthy people, into monsters who abused victims with terrible
cruelty. Despite Hitler's belief in eugenics, the SS commandant
was not a specially bred creature, but a perverted regular human
being. Many of us would doubt that we could choose to commit
one of the worst types of crimes against children, for example
rape of a young girl. Does that mean that someone who does
commit such a crime cannot choose the nature that drives them to
it? Or are they left having to constrain an evil impulse which the
rest of us neither experience nor understand and therefore have
no compassion for? Our view of choice here radically alters our
response to criminality and its treatment regime. We all have to
be philosophers and we have the responsibility to try to be good
ones.

Choice is therefore either non-existent or limited. Maybe it is a total delusion. But maybe it exists around the margin and as theories in areas like economics have shown, it is the marginal that is determinative, the tail that indeed wags the dog. The universe is contingent – it all depends on something. So choice and cause remain incompatible.

What about chance? This complicates the cause and choice debate even further. A cause does not directly lead to an unambiguous result. It might lead to a range of results dependent on a probability distribution. The existence of probability argues against teleology or purpose in the universe. Not all relationships are probabilistic – some are deterministic so that experiments can be repeated always with the same result. However, Karl Popper describes 'A World of Propensities' in which 'the world is no longer a causal machine – it can be seen as a world of propensities, as an unfolding process of realising possibilities and of unfolding new possibilities'. This open world Popper says is 'inherently creative'. 'There is no determinism in Newton's falling apple if we look at it realistically...because of the probabilistic character of the biological processes'.

The 'Copenhagen' theory of quantum mechanics pioneered by Niels Bohr introduced probability into the determinism of classical Newtonian physics. David Bohm, following Einstein who emphatically stated that 'God does not play dice', disagreed with this and developed a competing deterministic theory of the quantum atomic particle. Nevertheless, Bohm accepted both non-locality and the wider existence of stochastic phenomena exhibited as probability distributions. Contingencies always have impact beyond any system we may be studying or involved with. It is an unexplained reality that probability distributions pervade our experience of the physical world, not only in tossing coins, but for example in the distribution of height in the human population. It might be possible, if we knew all the causal variables fully, to explain any one person's height in terms of parental height, diet etc. But what we cannot explain is why the heights of everyone in the population follow an exact 'normal' probability distribution. Karl Popper was also fascinated with this and proposed that 'propensity', his refinement of probability, is a fundamental metaphysic of the world, alongside force and field. Newton discovered gravitational force, his formula measured it, but he could not explain it. Bishop Berkeley famously complained about the occult nature of this force. Maxwell, Faraday and others discovered the electro-magnetic field, another metaphysical. Popper suggested adding 'propensity' to recognise the pervasive presence of chance. This leaves us with cause, chance and choice mapped alongside the metaphysics of force, field and propensity.

Nathan Rosenberg in his 'Technology and the Wealth of Nations' describes the 'path dependent' view of economic and industrial development. Each of us realises that our present existence and life situation are the result of a chain of chance events. The cause is known - I exist because my parents met and reproduced - but there is huge factor of chance behind this chain of causal events, rendering cause non deterministic. Cause explains but only partially. It requires chance as its explanatory partner. Cause offers outcomes but does not determine them - chance becomes determinative. This is formally recognised in the mathematics of economic models - the random 'error' term is the basis of statistical theory used in estimating relationships between economic variables. We live in a stochastic world. Probability theory is usually introduced and its concepts developed through examples of tossing coins and throwing dice. But this is only illustrative and heuristic as a way to conceive the systemic nature of probability - probability as the major factor of our world paradigm. If cause and explanation was thought to remove God, how much more does the prevalence of probability challenge the possibility of a purposive God?

Determination of outcomes

What therefore are the determinants of the outcomes of life? A shortlist of potential determinants of any outcome could include

competitive capability

This is the Darwinian determinant and it has force as an explanation of events. At human sexual intercourse several million sperm are ejaculated and only one can possibly fertilise the female egg. The successful one may be the fittest (although we have to take care to avoid a tautology of success and best here) but other factors might also be at work

chance

This is the theory of the survival of the luckiest, the U term in statistical regression analysis, and Popper's 'propensity' metaphysical. It may turn out to be a very large percentage determinant of many outcomes we encounter. For example, was Microsoft the best operating software tool in the competitive market or did the wheel of chance and a few other factors lead to its near total dominance?

cause, logic and analysis

The Enlightenment advances logic and rationality as the determinant of outcomes. Everything is caused by something and causes something else. But business people are well aware that however logically a competitive product market is analysed, and however rigorously logical their decisions and actions are, the outcome may literally defy logic, again because other factors are at work

power

In a feudal society or a dictatorship, power determines outcomes more than competitive capability, chance or logic. Caesar decides. In contemporary world society there are many contexts where the person with the most crude power determines outcomes, whether they are logical or not.

desire and choice

Usually there has to be a huge wish from some actors for any outcomes to occur.

the status quo

Inertia is a powerful factor determining a huge number of outcomes, possibly the majority. The current outcome either equals or is heavily determined by the previous outcome. Path dependent theory is important in industrial market and general business analysis.

We see that we already have 6 major factors interacting to determine human and social outcomes. This analysis does not include God, but also limits the explanatory power of Darwinian theory and of Enlightenment logic. Feudal power, chance, human desire and the status quo are equal determinants of outcomes and therefore of the universe we live in. Cause, choice and chance interact to confuse and complicate the Enlightenment's simple trust in logic and reason.

In tracing its holistic history, we have thought about whether humanity is all and only physical, or has some metaphysical mind, soul and spirit, and if so whether this is separate, or integrated to the physical and dependent on it. We have tended to accept the physicalist view of the world but retained the view that this physical does generate and host mind, soul and spirit even though it may all one day get switched off together. The important acknowledgement of the metaphysical in human existence will lead to new potential for religion as myth to inform metaphysical life. But first we need to look at how far developments in cosmology point to the existence of some exogenous theistic entity, some God of the equations.

Are we alone? Does cosmology suggest theism?

So, based on our discussion so far, we remove an external God. This still however leaves an external world determined outside ourselves which we encounter and live in and with. The nature of this cosmos is fascinating and under continual exploration and discovery. The main question is whether the cosmos itself suggests, if not a designer, then at least a grand mechanic? Even if we maintain an impersonal explanation for why the material universe works as it does, it nevertheless exists exogenously to humanity and the mathematics of its operation appear to be exogenous too. Unlike the US astronaut Neil Armstrong, we may not find God by looking at it, but we do find a system, rules and logic defined and existing independently of us. Paul Davies in his 'The Goldilocks Enigma' gives an accessible account of the swirl of current understanding, hypotheses and uncertainty about the cosmological universe.

At the macro level the planets spin on their axes and trace their trajectories. Their universe is ever expanding, driven by an antigravity force which leaves the gravitational force between planets balanced by the mass energy within them. At the micro level, organic cells comprise sub-atomic particles which also spin, apparently at the same speed. Newton measured the force between objects in the universe and showed its proportionality to the product of their masses and the square of the distance between them. Important as this was, it only showed the relationship between the gravitational force and the mass of objects and the distance between them. It did not explain the mechanism of gravitational force which Descartes had previously speculated about with his 'vortexes'. Einstein demonstrated how light curved round planets and correctly predicted the orbit of the planet Mercury.

Quantum physics and particle physics took the theorising further. Particle physics identifies a wide range of particles – positrons which don't last long since they disappear if they collide with a neutron, muons which only last a few microseconds before changing into electrons or positrons, neutrinos emitted by the sun, billions of which pass through the human body every second. They all have the same level of positive or negative electric charge, or none at all, each has a corresponding antiparticle, all spin with a speed which is a multiple of ½ ! They are all made from quarks. The Large Hadron Collider currently being restored at CERN laboratory near Geneva hopes to identify the Higgs field and the Higgs Boson particle by replicating the moments after the Big Bang. Strings of particles lead to current developments in 'string theory'. Gravitation, electromagnetism and weak and strong nuclear forces hold the universe together, these forces probably resulting from an exchange of particles. The particular strength of these forces is essential to life as we know it and any small change might make the universe sterile.

Davies points out that whilst Darwin and Dawkins may have explained complexity without design in biology, the appearance of design in cosmology has not been explained. Attempts to do so are quasi Darwinian in positing multiverses which are subject to selection. For Davies the 'absurd universe' which is an inexplicable and random universe is unconvincing. So is the 'unique universe' which will be understood once a satisfactory unifying theory of physics has been discovered. He is equally unattracted to the multiverse theory and to the theory of intelligent design, preferring some 'self explaining' universe driven by a 'life principle' which is left only vaguely defined.

There are two immediate differences between this cosmos and humanity which inhabits a very small part of it. One is infinity and the other is purpose/meaning. Whilst it seems to be the case that the universe is infinite both in space and time, the human brain is finite in its operating mode and finds it difficult to conceive of something that goes on forever. It's incomprehensible to us that however small the chance of something occurring, in an infinite universe it will occur an infinite number of times. So there are an infinite number of each of us out there doing exactly what we are doing right now, a conclusion which seems absurd! The caution is that a finite operating mode brain cannot be used to comprehend infinity so the conclusion may be wrong and certainly feels that way.

Equally but as opposite, the universe has no purpose or meaning whereas humanity clearly does. Rather than struggle with these two asymmetries it's better to simply accept them and work within them. Applying the finite human brain to infinity is like trying to climb Everest on a bicycle. This doesn't mean that we shouldn't try since it's the only tool we have. But we will find disappointment if we look to the cosmos or indeed to anything outside ourselves for our purpose and meaning. We are free and able to define purpose and meaning for ourselves. Why do we want it to be externally developed and then imposed on us?

Since the human brain is purpose aware it can be purpose creative. This view liberates, but at the same time brings responsibility as well as opportunity. Even the religious view believes that its God placed humanity on earth and then gave a free remit. It's interesting that some people seem more intent on purpose than others. Some seem content to get on with life, others are keenly aware of the meaning and purpose of their life. Some are neurotic about it to the point that the awareness becomes counterproductive. What accounts for this psychological difference?

If we are not constrained in what purpose and meaning we choose to define, what constraints are there on us in the cosmos we live in? Clearly there are constraints of space and time metrics. But there also appear to be constraints of mathematics and logic. To the frustration and annoyance of the post modern philosopher, the system of logic seems to be set externally to us and we can't contradict it. But is this so? It seems to be, since the concept of infinity clearly exists in mathematics and logic, but cannot have been extrapolated from the human brain which cannot easily accommodate infinity never mind be capable of generating it. From Plato, through Immanuel Kant, and a range of philosophers of mathematics including Gottlob Frege, Kurt Goedel, Bertrand Russell, Ludwig Wittgenstein, David Hilbert, Paul Benacerraf, Michael Dummett, Michael Resnik, Charles Parsons, Crispin Wright and Stewart Shapiro, the question of the separate existence of mathematics and logic exogenous to humanity has been debated alongside the question of the separate soul.

Kant sought to harmonise the requirement that mathematics should be both 'a priori', existing in its own right, and yet also applicable to reality, but he could only do this by relying on 'intuition'. A great deal of subsequent mathematical thinking then sought to achieve this reconciliation without resorting to Kant's intuition. Mathematical realism required that mathematical entities corresponded to real objects, whereas Platonism allowed them to be abstract and not necessarily to correspond to any real entity. Mill's empiricism led him to claim that all mathematical concepts corresponded to a real object which they clearly cannot - negative numbers for example are useful abstractions for mathematical manipulations but negative quantities do not exist in reality. Does human cognition conform to objects or objects conform to human cognition? The great question was well phrased in the title 'Is Logic Empirical?' addressed by mathematical philosophers Hilary Putnam and Michael Dummett. Putnam followed work by Birkhoff and von Neumann to show that physical quantum measurement coded exactly like classical logic, leading to the view that logic is therefore empirical, exogenous to the human brain, separately existing, being discovered rather than invented by humans. Dummett showed that this invalidated the principle of distributivity and so was not indisputably so. Quine maintained that logic is subject to empirical revision.

Reading through the various schools of philosophy of mathematics including 'realism in truth value', Platonism, empiricism, anti-nominalism, working realism, rationalism, formalism, fictionalism, logicism and structuralism, the majority conclusion is that mathematics is exogenous to humanity, is discovered rather than invented. Stewart Shapiro, a leading figure in the contemporary 'structuralist' philosophy of mathematics, in his 2007 paper 'The Objectivity of Mathematics', tests a set of criteria for the objectivity of mathematics proposed by his fellow mathematician Crispin Wright in a 1992 paper entitled 'Truth and Objectivity'. Shapiro's conclusion is that mathematics does pass Wright's tests for objectivity, and so does exist outside humanity, is 'mind-independent', mainly because not all mathematical truths are 'knowable'. Mathematics, writes Shapiro 'feels more like discovery than invention', although he admits this could simply be a prejudice. Other alternative anti-realism and fiction-alist thinking by philosophers including Dummett, Field, Brouwer, Heyting and Yablo is that mathematics is independent of the physical world and all takes place in the human brain - it is an invented abstraction and is therefore separate from the physical world.

But how does this account for the formula for the roots of a quadratic equation being $x = \frac{-b \pm \sqrt{b^2 - 4ac}}{2a}$ or for π having a value of 3.14159... and being the link between the radius of a circle and its circumference and area, or between the radius and volume of a sphere? Or $e=mc^2$, or gravitational force being proportional to mass and inversely proportional to the square of distance? Or the gravitational force between two objects each of 1Kg placed one metre apart being 6.673×10^{-11} $m^3kg^{-1}s^{-2}$? Is 3.14159.. programmed in all human minds or does this geometric relationship exist whether humanity exists or not? Other metric relationships cited by Paul Davies are

- the distance a falling object travels increases as the square of the time it falls
- the force between two magnets diminishes as the square of the distance between them
- from Kepler that the square of the period of a planet's orbit is proportional to the cube of the orbit's radius
- and of course from Newton that gravitational force is proportional to the product of the mass of two objects and decreases with the square of the distance between them

Just as with complexity in biology, this mathematical metric regularity, this conformity to parametric laws may or may not suggest pre-existing intelligence in the universe. It is certainly more difficult to explain than the evolution of species by proliferation and natural selection which Darwin formulated. It is a mistake to assume that this universe is necessarily benign as the Goldilocks concept suggests. Meteors can be, have been, and may be again, very malignant. Tsunamis can kill multitudes. In this sense the cosmos seems to be value neutral, just as the biological world is, with its combination of creation and destruction. Neither therefore evidence a benign creator, or at least not one who sticks around to handle the consequences of the creation.

The point of this diversion into the complex world of cosmology, mathematics and logic is itself simple. The apparent order of the cosmos and the apparent exogenous reality of mathematics and logic, can be read to imply a designer, mechanic or at least some external specifications to the cosmos we exist in. This doesn't equate to Christianity's God but it does suggest some variant of theism, one whose god is restricted to an initial specifier of codes and logical rules.

Metaphysics – from Aristotle to Hegel

We live in a physical world and current intellectual physicalism rests on the hypothesis that there are no 'qualia', that everything is physical and that every apparently non physical phenomenon is mapped onto and generated by a physical host. There is no such thing as redness, only red things. But even if redness is totally dependent on red things and does not exist independently of them, still it exists as a metaphysical entity. It will disappear when all red things disappear but while they exist so does it. These were the concerns of Aristotle and other Greek philosophers in their definition of metaphysics. Aristotle also developed his concept of totality greater than its constituent parts which immediately generates a metaphysical.

Hegel and Durkheim built on this to show how social systems act in ways which make their totality greater than the sum of their parts, or in Durkheim's phrase 'reify' them, ie make apparent things of them. This is an important metaphysic. Institutions are one way in which society creates more than itself and can find itself bound by its own constructs, for example the law. It is possible for social organisations to take human societies in directions which none of the constituent members want. In this case a metaphysic is created and can be very powerful and effective. Hegel used Aristotle's concept of totality to justify the existence of the state which could act over and above the sum of actions of its citizens which was a necessary assumption for totalitarian state communism. The Nazi Third Reich had a destructive and awesome power of its own – its members could not restrain it even though they had created it. Such societal independent artefacts may rest on psychologies such as double entendre where atomised members thought that others thought or would act in certain ways, and this network of assumption, uncertainty, fear and insecurity, implicit rather than explicit, created a stronghold. But crowd psyche is similar and frequently observed in football crowd behaviour.

If Aristotle categories, Hegel totalities and Durkheim artefacts are physically dependent metaphysicals, then it is equally valid to allow the human soul similar physically dependent metaphysical existence. An idea is the product of the intellect and a feeling is a neurological phenomenon. Nevertheless both exist and so also does the soul.

Current thinking – the paradigm of postmodern society

The two important paradigms for humanity's self understanding today are those of modernity and post-modernity. We straddle the two and are transiting from modernity to post modernity.

Modernity enthroned reason and logic. Humanity could now become a much more productive producer. So the production and investment ethic thrived. Leadership was defined more by functional capability than by feudal power, although the two always co-exist and interact, vying for power. In modernity, function is more important than status, logic more important than power, content more important than image, working production known to be necessary for consumption.

However it is partly this huge productivity of modernity which has ushered in its successor paradigm of post modernity. In the age of abundance enabled by modernity, the logic/technology nexus seems less important and less interesting. A Marxist alienation has taken place. People do not know how the things they consume are produced. Neither do they understand the underlying fundamental technology behind the products they buy. Consumption has become detached from production. And consumption has become very brand aware. Not only must I have another pair of trainers, but they must be the right brand, the cool label. Heavy advertising has exploited the image conscious post modern human consumer to the full. What is being exploited is our own insecurity in our identity. We are no longer who we are but what we wear or what we drive. We have become far more conscious of our outer display than of our inner being and its qualities, its admixture of virtues and vices. The classical virtues are massively suppressed in post modernity. Being famous or being rich are the ultimate values. Being kind or generous doesn't get noticed, is not rated. These are qualities post modern humanity is hardly aware of, has lost sight of.

Status begins once again to dominate over function as democracy swings into 'celebrocracy'. Image becomes more important than content. It's very necessary to be 'cool'. Politicians are elected for their TV looks rather than the content of their manifestos. And naked power once again gains more respect than capable intellect or artistic performance. Education, which was prized in modernity, is devalued in post modernity or valued more for the doors it might open than in its own right. Consumption reigns over investment – the great Victorian initiated investment age where vast infrastructures of railways, sewers, underground metros, electricity grids were built has morphed into the consumption age where sleek cars, personal mobiles, TV and Internet devices, foreign holidays and all cool paraphernalia exclude attention to possible major leaps of imagination in creating new more environmentally effective infrastructures. Humanity is living on its past investments rather than creating new future infrastructures. Inherited wealth is an important aspect of the shift to post modernity from modernity whose paradigm created this wealth. The danger in this is that, as with the Roman empire, a consumer society may well yield to the philistines.

What therefore is humanity's current thinking? What is the predominant philosophy? One sad answer is that within post modernity, humanity is simply thinking less and focussing on feeling more. In UK culture, university graduates admit to reading few if any serious books in a year. Here logic is less valued as seen in discussion about whether to enter the Euro or to invade Iraq. Other cultures such as France contradict this trend with a high level of intellectual reading and a maintained interest in developments of thought which explains why the French joined the Euro and opposed the invasion of Iraq. The difference may well be due to the inclusion of philosophy in the French education system's baccalaureat and its exclusion from British school curricula. So whilst there is some embryonic new thinking and literature, for example on the philosophy of technology, a field which is so significant for humanity in reality that it should be attracting major new philosophical effort, most philosophy departments are content to reprocess what the classics thought. They are scribes, teaching from Aristotle, through Descartes, through Wittgenstein to Foucault, rather than creative thinkers themselves. Footnotes abound but new notes are rare.

The intellectual trend initiated by David Hume has largely concluded that humanity has no separate soul and is therefore wholly physical. Francis Crick who worked with James Watson to discover the double helix structure of DNA wrote in his 'The Astonishing Hypothesis' 1994 'You, your joys and your sorrows, your memories and your ambitions, your sense of personal identity and free will, are in fact no more than the behaviour of a vast assembly of nerve cells and their associated molecules'. The human soul passed from being an interest of theology through being a subject of philosophy to ending up a question for neuro-science. Physicalism dominates teaching and discussion in university philosophy departments. The essays on phenomenal consciousness and Frank Jackson's knowledge argument entitled 'There's Something about Mary' edited by Peter Ludlow, Yujin Nagasawa and Daniel Stoljar, generated huge debate on Jackson's question as to whether a woman called Mary, who had been given all physical knowledge but had been restricted to a black and white environment, would experience redness as a non physical 'qualia' on her release into the world of colour. The current conclusion of massive deliberation of this hypothesis by the world's philosophy community, including a repentant Frank Jackson, is that there are no non-physical qualia and the world is entirely physical. Therefore no separate soul, no religion, but interestingly fairly emotionally hostile attitudes (presumably not qualia?) to other hypotheses such as the much maligned Intelligent Design theorem which it's certainly cool to detest.

Where does the current synthesis of atheistic philosophy and post modern experience leave us? Post modernity has been interpreted into architecture, arts and literature. But its fundamental force is in reaction to the sovereignty of reason, logic and intellect established by the Enlightenment. It is therefore a shift in the holistic paradigm, pushing freedom and feeling to the fore of the human experience. Wind tunnel and computer CAD logic shows that there is one best shape for a new car design which is least drag, optimal power/weight ratio, and best ecologically, but I may simply not want this car shape imposed on me by rules of logic.

Post modernity is with us but is it here to stay? It has some fundamental weaknesses. It relies on the reason, logic and sheer productivity of the modernity which it eschews. Living by the feel factor will not generate much standard of living if logic is ignored. The overwhelming attention to image will falter if there is no corresponding content. Even the most cool advertising campaign will be sunk by a product which doesn't function well. And humility may once again become an appealing concept in a world overloaded with cult and celebrity status. The most serious defect of post modernity has already been mentioned – that the only alternative sovereign power to logic and reason is crude naked feudal power. We have been there before. There are real signs of this becoming the dominant power structure again. If politicians take the view that they can act irrespective of accountable rational justification, then feudal power is back. Our only hope is therefore to build a value system which has common appeal, and to which we yield sovereignty. This is where atheist conclusions and new interpretations of old misinterpreted religions may generate the synthesis we need.

The Church in Modernity

The church in modernity

(Let me insert a health warning. What follows in this section is a critique of church and its beliefs and practices. To repeat the TV mantra it uses strong language and may offend some readers. But its purpose and intent are not to offend. Rather it sets out an honest critique reached with some reluctance over time. Its aim is to make way for some other re-interpretations which appear in later chapters. I hope the reader will persevere to this later attempt at some reconstruction, if necessary by skipping the next chapter).

Where is the church in all this? How does it engage with humanity, with 'the culture'? Very little it seems. If there isn't a separate soul, there certainly seems to be a separate church. Its favoured communication method is the anachronistic unilateral one of preaching. Its sacramental practices are reserved for its clergy who dress differentially, almost druidically. Its idea of mission is for people to come to it and engage in unusual practices like community singing and embraces. Its message when it dares to enunciate it, which is increasingly less with time, is incomprehensible to the modern mind. It neither looks for nor welcomes critique, preferring to sink feeling itself unilaterally right rather than join in any embrace with its fellow humanity. Even when it does strip itself down to core mission in non church venues it is not looking for any debate, only to persuade of its increasingly unclear definitions of its faith.

There are three categories of church on offer – the evangelical doctrinal, the charismatic phenomenological, and the catholic ritualistic. Although different and in that sense diverse, still together they represent a very narrow engagement option.

The evangelical doctrinal offer is a strange hybrid. It starts by insisting that 100% of the Bible is 100% the authoritative word of

God. This starting point is open to all sorts of objection, but for this reason the evangelical church does not allow any objection. In some ways it is a distorted attempt to apply Enlightenment constructs of logic and explanation to its religion and faith. The result is a huge nonsense. Its founding leaders run from Luther and Calvin through to more recent 'systematic theologians' such as Louis Berkhof. In his 'Systematic Theology', Berkhof rearranged the Bible into a framework which created a story line with the bad news that all humanity has sinned, and a judgmental God has declared the eternal punishment of hell for everyone. However, the forgiving side of this same God who seems to have a seriously split personality, sent his son whose death on a cross was considered the penalty for all the sins of everyone ever. This creates the good news that if you know about it and believe it you get forgiven, get eternal life and will go to heaven rather than to hell. For those interested, key Bible texts for this formulation are in Romans 3:23, Romans 6:23 and John 3:16. Frankly it's bizarre and suffers from very serious shortcomings as an account of faith.

If God had wanted to say this, why didn't he just say it straightforwardly rather than it requiring the task of dissecting and reformulating the Bible? Starting with an insistence on infallible Bible authority is a tautology and intellectual nonsense, especially since interpretation of the Bible is so difficult and massively open to alternatives. Its utterly negative view of humanity is dire and sad, its doctrine of original sin unbalanced by any doctrine of original goodness. It owes more to its apostle Paul than it does to the discourses of Christ which have much greater moral appeal and challenge than evangelical doctrine, which has none. As Hyman Maccoby has pointed out in 'The Mythmaker : Paul and the Invention of Christianity', the core idea that a messianic figure came from another world and performed a human sacrifice so that only initiates in the religion would get salvation, is directly borrowed from the cult mystery religions of Paul's background in pantheistic Tarsus. It has no credibility for contemporary humanity but the evangelical church, including formally the Church of England, remains wedded to it.

Its core message of forgiveness is also so sadly distorted that it renders its particular brand of forgiveness morally repugnant, which is in itself an amazingly perverse achievement. Apparently, the evangelical's God only forgives if he can punish someone else, in this case his son. The historic motif for this idea comes from an earlier Bible story in which Abraham is supposed to have been told to sacrifice his son Isaac to God on Mount Moriah, and was commended for being ready to go ahead, until God provided a sheep in his place. The Danish theologian Soren Kierkegaard rightly struggled immensely with this perverted ethic in his 'Fear and Trembling'. The only interpretation by which this story can be rescued morally is that the Abrahamic God went to an extreme point to drill it into Abraham that he did not seek or sanction the child sacrifice commonly practised in other religions of the time. Judaism was to be different. But sadly this is not the interpretation the Bible itself takes of the story. Human beings *are* capable of the high ethic of forgiveness. It is rightly celebrated and held up as a virtue, as an objective for high moral behaviour. But it does not depend on beating up someone else. Such a crude view leads to a zero sum concept of forgiveness and has to be repudiated. In no other human interaction would it be considered acceptable – only by evangelical Christianity for its God. It has to be seriously reconsidered and abandoned and a more proper understanding of forgiveness formulated and declared worthy.

Another key deficiency alluded to by Comte-Sponville, is the evangelical claim of this God as father. Fathers vary in quality.

All of us by definition of being born had fathers of some degree of presence, however minimal, and some level of quality. Those of us who are fathers may seek to be good ones and might often regret not being better ones. The core concepts for a father are to provide, love, support, relate, lead and occasionally correct. God as father fails on many of these counts. He is absent and does not relate or answer. If he is there he plays some cat and mouse game. When my children call on the phone, I talk back to them. When they have a difficulty I go to them to see if I can help. Most human fathers do the same and some probably better than I do. Jesus compared the heavenly father God favourably to human fathers (Matthew 7:11). Sorry, but I would rate the human fathers I know as better than this deficient divine father.

The evangelical church is very aggressive. It argues adamantly for its belief both to the outside world and within its own fractured groups. It is characterised by being extremely sure of itself. It knows exactly what it believes, has formulated it in various creeds and statements of faith, and promulgates it. There is no room for doubt in its faith. It is exclusive, and indeed literally excludes those who do not share its precise specifications. Its internal divisions constantly multiply as it ever fractures over exactly what it believes over every possible theological detail. Currently the Church of England is on the edge of a worldwide split over subjects such as the sexual orientation and gender of its priesthood. Its internal discussions are hostile, and no example of grace in disagreement. It still excludes women from the role of bishop.

Previous disagreements were over even more arcane points such as whether Christ died for the whole world or only for the pre-selected elite, whether a thousand year period will precede or follow the return of Christ, whether a modern Christian can and should be 'baptised in the Spirit' etc. Its great bogeyman was the

Roman Catholic Church which it often vilified, opposing veneration of the virgin Mary, belief in transubstantiation of bread and
wine into the actual body and blood of Christ, supreme authority
of the Pope etc. Tracts were circulated including an infamous
tract titled '18 reasons why I am not a Roman Catholic'. Even
today a Roman Catholic cannot become monarch in the UK, and
no one appears sufficiently motivated to change this clearly
immoral legislation which flies in the face of other recent legislation against religious discrimination.

The evangelical church has its warrior movements including the
Evangelical Alliance, the Universities and Colleges Christian
Fellowship, and more to its credit the relief agency Tear Fund
which is part of the Evangelical Alliance. The exclusive detailed
basis of faith of the Evangelical Alliance can be read clearly on its
web site at www.eauk.org/about/basis-of-faith.cfm. The Alliance
makes it clear that this detailed statement of belief is one in its
own words 'which all Alliance members must subscribe to.' Its 11
points of belief major on themes of the Trinity, the Creation, the
Bible, universal human sinfulness, divine judgement, the
Incarnation, the atonement, justification by faith, the resurrection
of Christ, the Holy Spirit, the church and the second coming of
Christ. Only in point 11 is any ethical content included where
there is a fleeting mention of love and justice. Essentially this is
not a moral code but a highly precise statement of doctrinal
religious belief. The Evangelical Alliance considers that people go
to heaven by believing in these 11 points. They include no moral
requirement. They do not inform human behaviour at all. They
express a soteriological view of justice and no view of real actual
meaningful justice.

It is all not very far from the formulations of extreme Calvinists
who believe in five precepts of the total depravity of humanity,
unconditional election, limited atonement, the irresistible grace

of God and the perseverance of the saints. Even in its less severe forms this 'faith' is a set of theoretical concepts which have little or no implication in real life. They therefore fail the test of incarnation which is supposedly a major Christian interpretation and foundational belief. To the consternation of the evangelicals, their faith is in fact classic Gnosticism in that it offers salvation to select initiates who know the revealed knowledge, or to put it in modern simplicity, who subscribe to some codified ABC of salvation. Just believe and you are saved. People go to heaven just because of what they believe and go to hell if they don't believe it. Simple. Costless. And a very far fling from anything that comes anywhere near Dietrich Boenhoeffer's concept of faith set out in his 'Cost of Discipleship'. When one of its members Steve Chalke in his book 'The Lost Message of Jesus' questioned the centrality of 'penal substitution' ie the idea that Christ suffered punishment in the place of humanity so that humans could be forgiven, the Evangelical Alliance's reaction in defending this arcane and morally unjustifiable belief was huge and reminiscent of inquisition practice – see www.ekklesia.co.uk/content/news_syndication/article_ 041115_4754.shtml. According to Alliance spokespeople at the discussion the belief is foundational.

The Universities and Colleges Christian Fellowship (UCCF) has an almost identical statement of belief to the Evangelical Alliance (see www.uccf.org.uk/about-us/doctrinal-basis.htm). This organisation has as its objective 'making disciples of Jesus in the student world'. By this it means proselytising young vulnerable students, often away from home for the first time in their lives, and seeking to persuade them of this exclusive set of beliefs. It does this with a staff of 14 leaders and 59 field workers, which is a very powerful resource which it deploys among UK university campuses, and by which it controls their student Christian unions. This structure and practice are objectionable. In no other sphere does an external adult organisation have such a strong objective, and associated organisational resource, to deliberately seek to persuade students of its exclusive beliefs. There would be outrage if the Marxist Society did the same and campaigned so aggressively across all UK student campuses, and controlled its student groups so tightly. UCCF is not in effect a student expression. It is an external adult organisation which recruits and controls students. It does not stimulate intellectual debate and never sponsors open discussion, since it is dedicated to aggressively and determinedly pushing its own message. It even organises 'missions' to do this. Any attempts by real students to vary its themes and practices is ruthlessly crushed by its officers. This exclusive control is exemplified in the case of the Edinburgh student Christian union affiliated to UCCF who refused to invite the then Bishop of Edinburgh Richard Holloway to speak at its events because Holloway could not subscribe to their specific beliefs about the sacrificial atoning death of Christ.

In all this it is strongly differentiated from local university town churches many of whom thankfully adopt a non-militant support role to students in a context where Christianity is offered without being pressed and is not so rigorously and exclusively defined. Student life should classically be a time for open thinking about all aspects of life, academic, intellectual, personal, social, human, relational and holistic, and not one where students are prey to well organised vultures. It is sad that such pressure should be exerted on vulnerable students by organisations which are not prepared to engage with more equally equipped adults in general life. They know that the reaction from the more mature intellectual population is more sceptical and robust which is why they continue the strategy to 'get them while they're young'.

Some of this is slowly becoming uncertain ground for evangelicals as they personally, and their thinking and beliefs, mature.

The first casualty of belief is usually that of hell. The idea that a loving God can invent some eternal furnace and consign anyone who doesn't believe in his specific salvation scheme in it is too horrendous for modern evangelicals. In this rare case for an evangelical doctrine it does have implications, namely that the pleasant family next door who aren't evangelical Christians are in fact going to spend eternity this way. The very people they chat to happily and sometimes share a family barbecue and the school ride with! Evangelicals have therefore pulled back from this by suppressing it or re-interpreting the sayings of Jesus about hell as parable. This is a big step for evangelicals but they haven't grasped how big a step it is because, if parable is the correct interpretation of Christ and his teaching, then much more of their amoral literalism collapses in favour of more morally rich parable.

It would be unfair at this point not to include mention of TEAR Fund, the Evangelical Alliance's relief agency. TEAR fund carries out relief work worldwide and is a significant agency working to alleviate poverty. Its web site at www.tearfund.org puts far more emphasis on what it does and what its values are rather than what it believes. You have to dig rather more deeply to find its statement of belief and when you do it is more gently expressed and less exclusive and strident than those of its parent and sister organisations – see www.tearfund.org/webdocs/ Website/So F%20and%20S%26Cs/Statement.pdf. Its work is widely and rightfully commended and does represent a potential joining point of connection between the church and wider society.

However for a wide range of more general reasons, the evangelical doctrinal church's menu is not acceptable, believable or engageable for humanity today. There is as a result an unbridgeable chasm between this dominant sector of church and contemporary culture. This does not mean that contemporary culture does not want, seek, or need some belief system. It just means that it cannot find it in the evangelical church and must either look elsewhere, or construct one itself.

A development from this was the charismatic church offer. When pushed, it will assent to all the evangelical church's belief system, but it often soft pedals on this in favour of an emphasis on spiritual phenomena. It takes the Bible's description of the early church receiving the Holy Spirit, sees that this was accompanied by a host of 'signs and wonders' such as physical healings, speaking in tongues, prophecies, etc, and then seeks to replicate this experience. It imported Pentecostal church practices into the mainstream Christian church denominations. It proved very attractive and appealing for a time. Unemotional stiff upper lip Brits were able to find release and gladly clapped, sang and danced in anticipation of these spiritual phenomena. Documented healings however turned out to be scarce and well known leaders of the movement died despite intensive prayer for their healing. There is nothing more sickening than watching some evangelist/healer drag an elderly person from their wheel-chair in a public session and claim that they are 'healed' only for them to go home and remain wheelchair bound.

Its other phenomena either faded or became wacky – well known London Anglican churches were casting out demons from people who barked like dogs or flapped their wings like seagulls. Needless to say this did not prove sustainable. Sadly it seemed that the Holy Spirit could not or would not heal the sick today as He had in the New Testament, but He could be regularly relied on to pull off some lesser tricks like causing people to swoon and fall over, or to laugh uncontrollably for long periods, or even to be bodily catapulted across meeting rooms. Whilst the annual evangelical Spring Harvest conference is sympathetic to the charismatic wing of the church, it has been at the annual New

Wine conferences that these charismatic phenomena have been given their full head. Its leaders like David Pytches, a former missionary bishop to South America, toured the world and imported the latest charismatic manifestation from California, or in one specific case from a church in Toronto, and then through their conference disseminated these practices to local charismatic churches in the UK.

Not only did all this not offer a credible way into any belief system for secular humanity, but it actually did the opposite and led some previously inside church belief to conclude that it was no place for them. As with all charismatic movements, charismatic personalities dominated, and in the worst cases became demagogues, setting up strong authority structures and generally living well from them. This drove the movement into the shadows, yet further away from public access.

However within the Anglican charismatic movement, a more sympathetic and less intensive view of evangelical faith is marketed (literally) by the Alpha course developed by Holy Trinity church Brompton Road in London, see http://uk.alpha.org/. Whilst being friendly, more open to dissenting views being expressed in its sessions, and unthreatening to participants compared to traditional evangelical mission, it still focuses on theologies of the person and work of Christ and on personal salvation, deliverance and healing, remaining therefore Gnostic and consumerist. Ethics, social and political issues play no part in its agenda. And its optional weekend away puts some considerable pressure on attendees to have an experience of the Holy Spirit with the usual range of bizarre manifestations.

The catholic church emphasises belief less and membership of and adherence to church more. It is on the one hand more sympathetic to the human cycle of fault and restoration, but on the other hand totally blind to the suffering it heaps on the poor through its edicts against contraception. These simply get ignored in societies in modernity, but are obeyed in less developed societies with inevitable consequences of large low income families and deleterious effect on women's health. Amazingly this is all prescribed and enforced by a wholly male and moreover wholly celibate priesthood. This celibacy itself is a strange irrational denial of human sexuality, which by its suppression of reality has had sad consequences of distorted sexual abuse by priests in the Roman Catholic church causing major recent scandal. However at its best, the catholic church offering, because it focuses less on doctrine or phenomena, does lean more towards ritual which can match the human sense of glory and thereby have significant meaning.

The church gets revolutions wrong and ends up isolated and disconnected. It was wrong about the Copernican revolution – the world is round not flat, and it does go round the sun rather than the sun going round the world. The church's opposition to this, culminating in its excommunication of Galileo, made it and left it ridiculous. It got the sexual revolution wrong too, and has ended up irrelevant in an area where mature moral guidance is desperately needed. It insists that sex is reserved for married heterosexuals. Sex between any other couples in any other context is its prime definition of sin, and is most frequently what it has in mind when it uses the word 'sin'. In fact the vast majority of young heterosexuals have a sexual relationship before being married, and a large number of mature couples live together for some time before getting married, if they marry at all. Contrary to what the church says, this may have some virtue in that waiting for and therefore jumping into a sexual relationship for life at the point of marriage clearly carries considerable risk. Sex before marriage may be a wiser way than marriage before sex.

The technology has altered the morality. Before effective contra-ceptives, sex carried a strong possibility of pregnancy and a new life for the couple to be responsible for. This certainly constrains sex to a context where the responsibility for its possible outcome of parenting a new young life is accepted. But where contra-ception is available and effective this moral constraint is relaxed.

The Roman Catholic Church has at least maintained consistency here in that it refuses to sanction the use of contraception, so that sex always does carry the possibility for reproduction, and can therefore be argued to be necessarily restricted to marriage if marriage is defined as acceptance of and provision for parenthood. The Protestant church however is totally at sea. It allows that sex has value as an expression of love and can be disconnected from its reproductive role through contraception. It has thus sanctioned sex for pleasure but has formulated no new morality for this. Sex for pleasure clearly does not require marriage in the way sex for reproduction does. So having sanctioned the practice which sees the majority of teenagers engaging in sex or in a sexual relationship, the Protestant church has no ethic on offer and has in effect reneged on its role in society. It cannot offer any recommended ethic on teenage sex when it doesn't approve of it at all, even though it has supported the sexual ethic that has inevitably and logically allowed it. It then leaves secular society to struggle for a new ethic in this actual and widespread aspect of young human life.

And what could this ethic be? Is teenage sex always OK as long as pragmatics are respected, condoms used for the avoidance of pregnancy and sexually transmitted diseases? Is it OK to have sex with each and every boy/girlfriend as they come along? Or is sex a deeper expression – should it be respected as quintessen-tially holistic in nature and therefore be only where intellectual, emotional and relational bonds are in place? A well worn joke tells of a vicar speaking at a school on the ethics of sex. The vicar asks the pupils to consider whether it is worth risking happiness in future life for the sake of 10 minutes of momentary pleasure. Questions are invited and one girl puts her hand up and asks the vicar how to make it last for 10 minutes! The joke is slightly risqué but it sadly does capture an all too accurate picture of the divide in comprehension between the church and society on the vexed question of sexual ethics. The church bears responsibility for urgent reformulation. The greater likelihood is that it will shrink from this challenge as it does from so many others. It therefore guarantees its continuing and growing irrelevance, and its huge distance from secular life and its very real moral challenges. Other people have to make the difficult decisions which the church opts out of, preferring to stroke its precious conscience around the margin of life.

Even this very brief sketch review shows how the church has become alienated from the culture it is supposedly a part of. It can be a valued source of pastoral care and counselling, and it often does contribute to social programmes. But its belief systems are far away from most people's intellectual position. Having unpicked the knitting, there is little chance that they will become believed again. Only some fresh synthesis can hope to bridge this gap.

Towards a synthesis

Towards a synthesis – some connections

The physical connection

In seeking to build some synthesis, rather than set in concrete the growing complete separation of religion from today's culture, there are several strands of potential connection. It is very interesting that western Christianity is insistent on what it calls the Incarnation, ie any belief must be capable of being made physically real. It actually strongly rejects any belief system which is only spiritual, labelling it as 'Gnostic'. Its belief about Christ is very strictly that he came 'in the flesh' and its belief about his resurrection is that it was bodily and not only spiritual. These beliefs are outside the scope of most people today, but the emphasis on the physical is close to contemporary philosophy's view that the universe is totally and only physical.

The question for contemporary thought is whether it also defines any non physical elements. Are all feelings and emotions simply a collective effect of particle physics, for example the love of a person, the wonder at a symphony, the joy at a dance? Philosophers say that this is all dealt with in 'metaphysics', but a reading of the main available texts on metaphysics hardly confirms this. The metaphysics of Aristotle focussed on qualities - ie does redness exist or only red things? More meaningful questions are how to conceive of an idea, a perceived truth, a feeling, joy, love, sorrow, beauty, glory. There are non physical aspects to human beings even if they are powered by the physical and totally dependent on it. At the start of this book we took the idea of an idea. It seems fairly clear that ideas are somehow lodged in the brain. You can almost feel them there. Complex ideas can even make the physical brain hurt - the well known phenomenon of brain ache. Young babies have small brains and it is only when they grow in size that they can handle ideas. When people sleep, ideas become sub conscious, and when they die there are no ideas at all. It's fairly clear then that although ideas are non physical - they cannot be touched even at nano particle level - they do reside in the physical. This is evident from the example of writing. Physical ink is set out in agreed physical patterns on physical paper. But the physicality hosts another layer - the metaphysic of meaning. Moreover this meaning can now travel by physical light to the human eye where this meaning is decoded from the physical pattern and then communicated into the brain where it is registered presumably in some electro-chemical physical host. This idea can be forwarded to the mouth which can express the idea again in words which are agreed patterns of sound waves which transmit to another person's ear and are then registered in the receiving person's brain.

Furthermore, this verbal and written communication can lead to debate which can modify the idea which is then updated in the brain register. All this is pretty amazing and the mechanisms which enable it are hardly understood, even at the leading edge of neurological research. The best neurology is able to tell us is that certain areas of the brain appear to be responsible for certain categories of function. In summary however, we can agree that the physical human body's brain does generate the non physical of an idea. We can borrow from 'as if' methodology here and say that in our model of thought it is reasonable to regard ideas, feelings and emotions 'as if' they are non physical. The jury is out - they may eventually be shown to be entirely physical but it is equally likely that they are metaphysical products of the physical body. The latter feels the more compelling hypothesis from our present state of knowledge.

This physical / non physical connection is apparent in the vast array of psychosomatic interactions we experience, and in the stress on holistic understandings of human beings. We know that physical exercise releases anti-depressive chemicals which then inspire and refresh the mind. People can develop physical ailments from a negative state of mind, or can feel depressed due for example to a broken bone. Stress and anxiety can induce a wide range of disease including psoriasis, eczema, stomach ulcers, high blood pressure, and heart disease. More simply, sweating, palpitations, fast breathing, or a fast heart rate can all result from a mental state of anxiety. Thure von Uexkeull's 'Psychosomatic Medicine' sets out a very full range of psychosomatic disorders. Sex combines human physical and emotional elements powerfully. Tender feelings, relational attractions which are both physical and psychic, are expressed in physical embrace and tactile caress of sensitive body cells, leading to climactic physical explosion with overwhelming emotional feeling, the whole then subsiding into a calmer psychosomatic state. Sex is an interactive incarnation - feelings are expressed physically, and physical sensations generate huge feelings.

As we saw in our 'holistic history of humanity', human societies have tended over time to emphasise one partial aspect of the holistic totality. Plato considered the mind and the spirit to be the noble aspect of the human being, establishing the 'platonic' notion that bodily functions are all less worthy, less dignified and even an embarrassment. This has led to western society suppressing its awareness of body, feeling easily embarrassed, being less tactile, and generating a huge neurosis about sexuality which has in turn led to immense psychological disorder. Metaphysical concepts of guilt have mushroomed. There is something very uneasy about western sexual awareness. Young men reaching puberty are left to feel either guilty or randy about their inevitable erections and emissions. Women feel threatened if a man makes any approach, and eventually feel neglected if as a result none do. This is all due to the platonic distortion where spirit is refined and flesh is not. On the other hand, some societies regard emotion as a weakness. Men in particular should not cry. This leads to immense blocking of personality where now both flesh and emotion are suppressed. British society was famed for this dual suppression but has seen a great transformation as the stiff upper lip has morphed to the touchy feely society showing how swift such swings can be.

The more complete human being has an ease in holistic awareness, acceptance and engagement. This involves both care and use. To eat well, to exercise, to enjoy sport, to maintain physical strength and capability whilst also developing intellect, interest, intelligence and knowledge, whilst also expressing mature feeling whether positive ones of love, joy or managing negative ones of anger or sorrow - this multi-dimensional whole is humanity, and every human being has the potential to grow fully in each.

The soul connection

In the same way, human beings do think of themselves as having a soul. Sometimes this is felt to be in the brain, but interestingly can have other psychosomatic connection to the stomach or the heart, which is where other philosophies located their soul. Non physical feelings can generate physical feelings. Let's accept that David Hume and the Hume school of thought were correct, and that there is no separate soul. Just as ideas reduce with sleep and die at physical death, so do feelings. It is self evident to any parent watching a baby grow through young childhood that physical brain growth is the enabler of ideas and feelings. A baby may have Freudian feelings and thoughts and long for womb security, adopt a foetal position, or remember its mother's heartbeat. A one year old communicates basic desires for food and sleep and complains against pain. A two year old expresses this through basic language. By the age of five, reasonably complex ideas are possible. But it's not until teenage years that the brain can cope with mathematical formulae, abstract reasoning and appreciate literature, art and music. All this capability is clearly dependent on growth of brain size and function. Since the metaphysics of intellectual and emotional capacity are very definitely physically dependent, then it is not unreasonable to assume that any soul or spirit is also a physically dependent metaphysic and does not have separate or eternal existence. But neither does it mean that it lacks existence at all – it is simply that it is a physically dependent existence.

The human brain is a remarkable instrument. Its functions are little understood by modern neuroscience whose state of development is similar to the first maps of the world produced by the early explorers. Neuroscientists can tell roughly what areas of the brain account for which functions. Curiously the brain appears to be able to conceptualise widely, and even to generate the phenomenon of human consciousness, but at the same time it has two limitations – it cannot yet understand itself, and it cannot understand the infinity which is the context in which it exists.

However the important point in building some synthesis is that an agreement that the soul is not separate and does not exist in eternity does not mean that the soul doesn't exist at all. Current atheist thinkers and campaigners do not deny the existence of the mind, so why deny the existence of the soul? We can agree that it may well be entirely powered by the physical body and will not survive the death of that body, but this still leaves us with soul and acknowledges that humans have spirit. The problem with the atheist formulation is that it is entirely destructive. It offers no other understanding of humanity than that all is physical, there is no God and no separate soul. Somewhere in this gap we have to find a meaningful understanding of who we are as beings who are clearly aware of meaning.

The divine connection

Observation of the universe and humanity within it may well have led us to the conclusion that there is no God. That is that there is no external exogenous being acting outside and independently of humanity. No one who preceded us, no one who created us, no one who cares for us, no one who prescribes for our life. Fine. But what then? If there is no Divinity, does it mean that there is no divine? We can use the word divine quite casually, for example to refer to a cream cake or some wondrous music. But we can equally use the word with more significance to our values. For example we often say that it is human to err and divine to forgive. I want to suggest taking this use of the word divine and building on it. Let's say that it is indeed divine to forgive. What other behaviours, qualities, conditions, responses, graces would we want to include as divine? The Christian apologist C S Lewis objected to the phrase that 'love is God' because he insisted on the theist view that the thought was the other way round, since as the Bible says, 'God is love'. That may be a nice trick to create space for a God belief, but he was not at all necessarily right in rejecting the more obvious connection. So far we may have agreed that forgiveness and love are divine. We might add the other classical virtues celebrated by Andre Comte-Sponville in 'A Short Treatise on the Great Virtues' ie politeness, fidelity, prudence, temperance, courage, justice, generosity, compassion, mercy, gratitude, humility, simplicity, tolerance, purity, gentleness, good faith, and humour.

We may reject or simply not have found a God, we may reject imposed belief or value systems, we may believe that we are only physical beings, but we are still able to accept that our physical does generate a metaphysical mind and a metaphysical spirit and that from them we are able to determine what is divine. Contemporary philosophers suggest that humanity has the responsibility for defining its own world, but then shrink from any assistance in that task. There is therefore a potential synthesis here. Religion may have to shed its doctrinal framework, forget its phenomenological baggage, and minimise its ritual, but then it may be able to assist in defining a divine which is on offer for life and not at all imposed. People can subscribe to this divine as they want, but every indication from the burgeoning expressions in the blog world is that most people would subscribe to a divine that included for example justice.

The virtues defined as divine then have to be regarded as ruling virtues. We are free to agree that the Comte-Sponville list of virtues constitute our divine - we subscribe to them, we obey them, we allow them to rule real situations, to determine our life and our life choices, to be celebrated and upheld in our communities. We can choose this divine and submit to it. Strangely though, Comte-Sponville himself is a determinist and doesn't think that we can choose anything, including the great virtues he so wonderfully extols. Our scope for choice is thought through in an earlier chapter.

The myth connection

Myth is traditionally a weak word. Oh, we say it's only a myth, it's not true, it won't happen. Hyman Maccoby derided the apostle Paul as the 'Mythmaker'. But I want to argue that myth is a powerful word. There is of course something arbitrary about a myth - it can be created to convey good or bad ideas and intent, it can liberate or constrain, instil hope or fear. Religions in fact include multiple myths, but religious people eschew the idea of myth. Instead they insist on making literal truth from what was originally myth, and think that they have thereby strengthened the myth to a truth. And woe to any who don't believe this truth. A sad example is from Hindu belief. The myth of Rama and Sita is beautiful, appealing, and offers moral virtue. Rama and Sita are married and live in a forest. But the demon king Ravana tricks Rama away with a demon deer so that he can kidnap Sita in his winged chariot. Sita drops a trail of her jewellery for Rama to follow and he then meets Hanuman the monkey king who gathers 23 million monkeys to look for Sita. Hanuman finds Sita as Ravana's prisoner on an island surrounded by a raging sea. A great army of monkeys, bears and squirrels build a bridge to the island to rescue Sita. After a pitched battle Rama fights Ravana and after failing to kill him by cutting off his many heads, eventually slays him with an arrow made by the sky god. Rama and Sita return home and live happily.

So good triumphs over evil and the lights that people light expel all the darkness. So far so good. It's similar to myths in other religions and to morality plays in secular theatre. But, and it's a big but, the value of this myth is lost when Hindu religion turns it into a literal belief. Seeing doll like statues of Rama and Sita in small dolls' houses trivialises the great myth. The same is true of the wide panoply of moving Hindu myths. Sadly people seem discontent with myths and insist on their literalisation. But they miss the point. There is no sadder contradiction than that from a visit to Ayodya in India. Here is the city with the greatest number of Hindu temples in India. Up to 1992 there was also one mosque. But this was burnt down, an act which caused ricochet riots and burnings across India. Now visitors can follow a military guarded fenced walkway to see this disputed site. There they find the rubble of excavation to discover whether the site was originally Moslem or Hindu, although the historical answer is obvious and well known, and perched on this rubble are two dolls in a dolls' house to represent the gods of Rama and Sita. What a travesty this is from the beauty of the originating myth. Of course it's not only Hindu religion which inherits great myths and turns them into trivial beliefs. It is doubtful that Buddha wanted to bequeath golden statues of himself for worship in temples. An Anglican clergyman related an occasion when he addressed a retreat conference on the story of Jonah who the Bible says was swallowed and later disgorged on a beach by a huge fish. One group member was insistent that the clergyman accepted the literal historical truth of this story and left the group in disgust when the clergyman appeared ambivalent on this point. Myths can convey great moral aspirations and hope and so have huge potential impact for humanity. On the contrary, belief in the literal event can have no significance at all, cannot pass the 'so what?' question, is essentially meaningless.

A proposed synthesis

Two of the atheist writers cited so far end their books with a hope or search for some remnant or alternative spirituality. John Humphrys ends with a wistful hope that maybe doubt in God might leave some possibility of God. Andre Comte-Sponville's 'Book of Atheist Spirituality' develops an other worldly spirituality which reads attractively, if feeling rather inaccessible. Is there therefore some spirituality which can co-exist with an atheist position on the existence of an exogenous God? Can the sacred and secular meet? Can religious text open meaningfully for free exploration, fresh encounter and valuable interpretation? Can its poetry convey more meaning than doctrine and dogma which have been wrung from it? Can selective cherry picking yield valued insight and worthwhile inspiration? This exploration is the aim of the next chapter.

In suggesting elements for a synthesis which responds to the postulate of atheism with a reconstruction of spirituality, or at least with something worth believing, Voltaire's famous phrase 'Si Dieu n'existait pas il faudrait l'enventer' (if God didn't exist we'd have to invent him), admittedly taken out of context, suggests we do exactly that. Since God doesn't exist, let's invent our own. Or more seriously let's define divinity ourselves, some set of what is worthy, some ruling virtues for our life. This involves a re-interpretation of the idea of faith and a re-interpretation of religious texts specifically including the Bible. This re-reading emphasises myth as the meaningful interpretation against literalism, doctrine or creed. It deliberately allows cherry picking, taking meaning where it offers virtue, and leaving aside or rejecting text at will. It clearly therefore attaches no a priori status or authority to the text. It is not the word of God, but it might be valuable, and where it is we'll take that value and use it to help construct our preferred divine.

It is clear that the Bible has become a closed book in contemporary society. Awareness of its content and potential is at an all time low. In previous generations the Bible has had a very strong effect on society. Christopher Hill in 'The English Bible and the Seventeenth Century Revolution' traces how the first English language Bible of 1611, through its denunciation of injustice of ruling monarchs, broke the 'divine right of kings' claim and led to the regicide of Charles the First in 1649. In total contrast in 1995 the Church of England, aided and abetted by various evangelical groups, successfully campaigned for legislation to prohibit the Bible from being read at civil weddings in the UK, which is not only an unacceptable act of censorship in a free democratic society, but another example of the church shooting itself in the foot and further widening the huge gap between itself and the society of which it is a part. Once again the church is master and not servant.

Secondly any virtuous re-interpretation of a religious text like the Bible is not unique. It stands alongside and synthesises with other texts, religious or secular in nature, with novels, films and all art. For example, Christopher Ricks' work 'T S Eliot and

Prejudice' is a major moral challenge on the subject of prejudice far beyond anything on that subject in the Bible, which tends on the contrary to be guilty of huge ethnic prejudice itself. Susan Neiman's 'Moral Clarity' includes a wonderful chapter on 'Hope' where she trounces the negative view of humanity shared by religion's original sin and evolution's selfish gene and follows primatologist Frans de Waal in claiming altruism as a fundamental human characteristic, feeding distributive justice in human society, and neurologist V S Ramachandran in observing 'mirror neurons' in the human brain which means we are 'wired up for empathy and compassion'. She triumphs the potential for heroism instead of resignation in individual living. Equally, great films, novels and plays like 'The Reader' on the perpetrator as victim, 'The Crucible' on religion as a cloak for perversity, 'To Kill a Mockingbird' on racial prejudice, 'Gandhi' on non-violent protest, Nathanial Hawthorne's 'Scarlet Letter' on religious hypocrisy or 'The Birthmark' his renowned early feminist work, all make powerful moral points. Nevertheless it's worth taking value from the religious texts where we can, as Susan Neiman does herself from the Biblical myths of Abraham and Job.

Andre Comte-Sponville
A Short Treatise on the Great Virtues

The contemporary expression of philosophy closest to a secular Bible is Andre Comte-Sponville's 'A Short Treatise on the Great Virtues' published in 1996. Comte-Sponville is a philosopher at the Sorbonne. His book achieved mass circulation and readership in France and has been translated into 24 languages. On a rather arbitrary basis which limits the book's standing as a work of overall philosophy Comte-Sponville selects 18 virtues each of which he then unfolds and celebrates. His great virtues are

- politeness
- fidelity
- prudence
- temperance
- courage
- justice
- generosity
- compassion
- mercy
- gratitude
- humility
- simplicity
- tolerance
- purity
- gentleness
- good faith
- humour
- love

Frequently quoting Aristotle and Spinoza but also often referring to the writings of Vladimir Jankelevitch and the French philosopher Alain, Comte-Sponville creates a compelling thought world of ethical virtues.

Politeness, courage, sympathy and tolerance, whilst celebrated, are ambiguous, and therefore insufficient virtues since they are 'blind to value'. They can serve good or evil. Politeness can be a false facade, and tolerance can be compromised, but they are both foundational virtues since they give respect to others. Even fidelity is suspect, unless the virtue one is faithful to is justified, or the commitment one is faithful to is human, particular and historical. Fidelity is to values, and cannot be to feelings or to specific relationships which can evolve into new unforeseen contexts and realities. Prudence makes us consider and be responsible for the consequences of our actions and not only their intentions. Crucially it guides us in how to implement the other virtues.

Temperance allows us to master our pleasures and not to be their slave. It is the art of enjoyment. Comte-Sponville quotes from Montaigne 'excess is the pest of pleasure, and self restraint is not its scourge but its spice'. Courage is virtuous in mastering fear, especially fear of suffering. It is the readiness to take pain for what is right or what must be done. It is strength in despair against all hope. Humility is not a low view of self but a sufficiently non inflated view of self to admit 'I may be wrong'. Simplicity is to be at peace with oneself and with one's context, although discontent can be creative. Pity includes trace elements of contempt and adds to total human sadness and so is not virtuous.

According to Comte-Sponville, morality is not absolute but is learned and so is described as 'first an artifice then an artefact'. Morality is only necessary where love fails. Love may generate generosity, but generosity does not per se generate love. One can decide to be generous but cannot decide to love, so in this sense generosity, being voluntary, is the greater virtue. Of generosity Comte-Sponville says 'its most beautiful name is its secret, an open secret that everyone knows : accompanied by gentleness, it is called kindness'. Generosity gives others more good than they deserve, whilst its corollary mercy delivers less punishment than is deserved. Love is tripartite. Eros is lack, generating desire for self fulfilment as in the fable of Aristophanes where Zeus cuts the whole person into two parts who must then regain union. Philia is mutual joy. Agape is selfless love of another. These love components are distinct but symbiotic – agape allows the love of enemies enjoined by Christ, but none of agape, philia or eros would lead to marriage between enemies. Selfless love is virtuous but has to start with self love, and indeed ultimately satisfies self love in the recipient beloved other.

The book is a discourse on virtue and as such is highly appealing. It fills a hole in the material consumerist atheist zeitgeist which accounts for its immense popularity. Reading it provokes thought and consideration about virtue. Contemporary western culture would be revolutionised for the better from widespread reading of this advert for virtue in place of its regard for the clamouring adverts for consumerism. Since it presents the virtues selectively and per se, the book lacks a philosophy or a theology. But this is also its advantage in that no overall scheme is being argued – just virtue, intrinsic virtue, which stands as a bottom up disaggregate philosophy itself. In some ways the book falls between two stools by being somewhat long-winded with frequent circuitous quasi academic references, whilst failing to satisfy the academic requirement for impenetrable syntax. Its curious nature however is that Comte-Sponville celebrates these virtues which partially describe how we could live well, and then declares himself a determinist. So here are beautific virtues beautifically argued for, but it appears they are outside our grasp since we are determined rather than cognitive decisive beings. Comte-Sponville does not address this paradox. Presumably we therefore either have to apply our cognitive powers to choose the way of these virtues in our lives, or else hope that reading Comte-Sponville is a determinist mechanism to them flourishing in our lives.

Another contributor to the debate on virtues in human society is Iain King. In his racily titled book 'How to Make Good Decisions and be Right all the Time' King, a UK Cambridge philosopher and colleague of Simon Blackburn, develops a methodology for moral decision making based on a net help calculation that the value of the help to someone else is greater than the cost to the helper. He derives this from two core virtues of empathy and obligation, which he claims drive all other virtues, although he does not demonstrate this. Similarly King casually dismisses the argument advanced inter alia by Matt Ridley that altruism does not exist, but itself has pragmatic drivers. This is surprising as, like Ridley, King appears to be searching for a humanist foundation for virtuous behaviour which does not rely on any divinely revealed code. He quotes heavily from John Rawls on justice but not from his critic Robert Nozick. For an erudite academic the argument is extremely cursory and the proposed methodology very simplistic. Can great moral dilemmas be so simply solved? Can objectivity be achieved in subjective valuations? And if so, how come no one realised this before King did? Indeed, due to well known difficulties in moral decision making which he gradually unfolds, King develops from 9 rules in chapter 22 of his book to 14 rules in chapter 30, and finally to 20 rules in chapter 38, only to admit in the next chapter 39 that in reality we face huge uncertainty about the outcomes of any course of action, about the value of those outcomes, and about the interpersonal weighting of these valuations, which invariably calls for judgment and wisdom, which most of us knew all the time.

Terry Eagleton in his 'Reason, Faith and Revolution' makes the startling pithy statement that 'there has been no human culture to date in which virtue has been predominant'. This is a huge indictment of human society in its past, and an equally huge challenge for its future. As a rare admixture of Catholic Marxist Eagleton refers to Thomas Aquinas whose view was that 'all virtues have their source in love'.

Having set out a secular contribution to the synthesis, we now look at the contribution religious literature can make to great ethical themes.

What follows is not an attempt to establish any belief. It is not intended at all to be prescriptive. It assumes no authority or status for any religious text. What is offered is a set of examples of how the use of myth as an interpretative paradigm of selected religious literature, in this case from the Judaic-Christian Bible, can yield light on a range of issues which secular society cares greatly about. If these examples work at all, then they constitute some basis for the synthesis between secular philosophy and religion as myth.

We start with justice.

Justice

Justice is a core rallying virtue for humanity. It is also the core Judaic and Christian vision and hope, the aim of all their histories, their governing virtue. Judaism and Christianity have misunderstood this and substituted other false concepts, core goals and ideas. Partly this has arisen in the English speaking world as a result of a semantic confusion. The Bible has a consistent vision of a kingdom being established - the kingdom of God, but crucially defined as a kingdom of justice. The Hebrew word 'tsedeq' and the Greek word 'dikaiosune' mean justice. But over 500 times these words are translated by the alternative vague spiritual English word 'righteousness' and only 140 times as 'justice'. They are in fact the same word in other languages - for example 'la justice' in French or 'Die Gerechtigkeit' in German. This has led to major consequences in the English speaking world. A doctrine of personal spiritual salvation has been constructed from the use of the word 'right-eousness' which itself it not understood outside this theologised church world and frankly hardly understood in any meaningful sense within it. However, substitute always the translation 'justice', and a whole new emphasis of meaning emerges.

Suddenly we have the injunction to 'look for the kingdom of God and his *justice*', this same kingdom is described as consisting of '*justice*, peace and joy', 'the result of *justice* will be peace' etc.

This 'religion' is suddenly political, suddenly social and economic and human. It's a very different, a much stronger, a totally more relevant spirituality. And a more costly one than simply believing some formula for personal salvation, which must be the weakest, feeblest, and most consumerist distortion ever wrung out of far stronger raw material. Judaism and Christianity can more properly be defined as a social justice agenda. The kingdom of God is a powerful myth for a just society. They not only establish this as the constant vision and goal for humanity, but they offer some moving insight as to how such a just society can evolve, as well as stating the conviction that it is ultimately inevitable.

A key principle repeated frequently in the Judaic Christian text is that justice is priority, and that it will almost automatically generate peace. Conflict and war whether between individuals or nations arises from injustice felt by one or both sides. The 'peace for our time' announced by Neville Chamberlain in 1938 failed because justice was ignored, utterly breached and displaced by atrocity of Hitler's regime. Peace in all conflict zones requires justice, and will never be established without it. Peace in the Middle East is a current priority. It will never be established by military imposition, but only by addressing the underlying causes of real and perceived injustice. Judaism should be more aware of this than seems to be the case, since it was Judah's prophet Isaiah who wrote that justice would be established in the desert as well as in the fertile field, and that its result would be peace and calm secure living (Isaiah chapter 32, verses 16-18). Their own psalmist expresses the poetry that 'justice and peace kiss each other' (Psalm 85 verse 10) and their prophet Malachi (chapter 4 verse 2) promises that 'the sun of justice will arise with healing in its wings'.

Peace is a natural inevitable consequence of justice, and conflict is an inevitable consequence of injustice. Justice will be more effective in securing peace than powerful military technology. For the believer and certainly for Judaism, their God leads in paths of justice (Psalm 23 verse 3). Justice is far more challenging than the personal righteousness of other weaker translations. Being 'right with God' is too easy an avoidance tactic for focussing on the more difficult challenge of being right with other people. Putting total emphasis on addressing justice for Palestinian peoples would move Israel rapidly towards the potential for peace in the Middle East. Israel's own scriptures tell it this, but it seems either not to know or not to listen. Again according to Isaiah, if Israel is considered special in any way, it is only in that it would be a model of justice for other nations to admire - 'he will make justice shine on the nations, never faltering, never breaking down, he will plant justice on earth' (chapter 42 verses 1-4 and chapter 61 verse 11), a calling it currently shows little concern for. Justice is antithetic to selfishness. It fundamentally requires concern for the other party. Where self interest becomes established, justice will suffer and conflict will be the likely outcome.

In Christian teaching justice is also priority. The poet Ezra Pound is said to have torn out of his Bible all the pages he didn't agree with, and this is said to have left him only with Christ's famous Sermon on the Mount which includes the beatitudes, or sayings of blessing, which themselves include the moving expression that 'blessed are those who hunger and thirst after justice for they will be filled' (Matthew chapter 5 verse 6). Every human rights activist should be inspired and encouraged by this. Conversely every Christian should be a human rights activist, since these concepts are core to a large part of Christ's teachings, sayings and parables.

According to Christ, activism for this kingdom of justice transcends all other material concerns (Matthew chapter 6 verse 33). G R Beasley Murray in 'Jesus and the Kingdom of God' demonstrates how focussed Christ was on this kingdom of justice and its centrality for human beings and human society. Beasley Murray expounds 16 sayings and 18 parables of Jesus on the kingdom of God, using metaphors of treasure lost and found, of mustard seed which grows slowly but immensely, of good prevailing over evil, of yeast, of mercy and justice in positions of authority, of talents used or buried. If we reject any authority for these texts, they are at least heuristic and inspiring.

It is true that the New Testament writer Paul often interprets this core concept more in terms of personal salvation. To him faith is needed to be given a righteousness which cannot be achieved by human effort. But this is spiritualised transcendence and frankly has little meaning. The greater interpretation is that the clarion call to justice is accompanied by a faith - faith that it can be so and ultimately will be so. Then the great Christian expectation might be realised that 'the kingdoms of this world have become the kingdom of our Lord and of his Christ and he shall reign for ever and ever (Revelation chapter 11 verse 15), or for Judaism from their prophet Daniel that 'his dominion is an everlasting dominion which shall not pass away, and his kingdom one that shall not be destroyed' (Daniel chapter 7 verses 13-14).

There have always been theories of history including Marx's and Vico's, but this Judaic Christian theory that injustice will not ultimately prevail, that human governments, dynasties and regimes will come and go but that justice will survive as the governing principle, is not only attractive but apparently real. The evil regimes of Hitler, Pol Pot, Idi Amin, the injustices of empire whether Roman or British, have indeed succumbed. The fight for a just society continues and the prevalence of a just society is notable. Justice is a social phenomenon - it only applies between people and never to an individual person. It confers equality of rights and some equalisation of excessively unequal incomes in society. It is not defined by authority or by military power - contrary to C Wright Mills' famed expression, might is not right. Neither is it determined by a democratic majority since recent history shows that a majority vote can even elect an evil regime.

The philosopher David Hume thought that five conditions caused justice to cease to have value. These were conditions of extreme abundance, universal love, extreme poverty or violence, unequal strength and power between people, and isolation of people from each other. His thinking on this was limited and wrong. Extreme abundance may eliminate economic or property injustice, but not for example the injustice of murder. Universal love or altruism may indeed seem to make justice redundant, but rather it may seek and implement a justice which still has to be defined. There is no reason why extreme poverty or inequality should render justice inoperative - quite the contrary as these conditions highlight the need for justice.

But justice does present a problem. It is indefinable! It is relative and not absolute. So scope for argument and continued conflict is apparent. In the Middle East example quoted above, Israel has the well understood complaint of the massive injustice, indeed the atrocity of the Holocaust. Palestinians have the strong complaint of injustice of displacement from much more recent homelands. In economic disputes the argument over what division of national income or company profits is 'fair' does not have one correct solution. In micro disputes between neighbours, colleagues or partners, a fair outcome is a relative judgment.

What is fair in economic society? How equal or how unequal should income, wealth and lifestyles be within one national society and between national societies across the world? Should the issue of equality be limited to opportunity and not to outcome, or include outcome as well? If two people had the same opportunity in life and one worked hard whilst the other lazed, or one had better luck and so became richer, should these incomes be equalised? Or adjusted to be more equal? Is it fair for the hard worker to be deprived of his/her income? And if they are, will they lose the incentive to work so hard? On the other hand why are the poor poor? Is it because of lack of effort, or lack of opportunity, or lack of gift, or lack of luck? Or is it because their output has been exploited by the rich and powerful, either through feudal force or by the sophisticated price system of a market economy? These are all difficult moral questions and the lack of a clear singular unambiguous answer shows how elusive a definition of justice is. Typical conservative 'right wing' attitudes emphasise the first set of points, whilst more socialist 'left wing' views embrace the latter ideas.

There is strong academic debate on the definitions of justice. John Rawls in 'A Theory of Justice' argues that 'social and economic inequalities are to be arranged so that they are to be of greatest benefit to the least advantaged members of society', his well known 'maximin' principle of distributive justice, whereas Robert Nozick in 'Anarchy, State and Utopia' regards unequal outcomes as just if they derive from equal opportunity starts and free exchange. Rawls was heavily influenced by Isaiah Berlin who regularly pointed out that moral objectives can sometimes clash, as for example the values of freedom and equality do – we cannot have both without constraint because freedom may very well generate inequality. There is therefore no unique overall moral absolute, no single definition of justice, even for this reason that values trade off against each other. Some hold the view that injustice only exists where a situation is enforced ; critics point out that entirely voluntary situations can still be defined as unjust. A further question is whether some relationship between parties is necessary for justice to be defined – is it unjust if two societies who have no contact with each other have very different standards of living?

The Nobel Prize winning economist Amartya Sen in his 'The Idea of Justice' argues with John Rawls' theory of justice in that it relies on just institutions working with a social contract towards a transcendental, ie potentially unachievable, vision of a perfectly just society. Sen critiques this for ignoring real actual achievable outcomes, excluding wider interests, and failing to address behaviour. He proposes instead that justice should operate by comparing actual outcomes through a process of unrestricted public reasoning. He offers one example, of whether a flute should belong to a child who can play it, a child who has no other toys, or the child who made it. His reliance on public reasoning is weak since he fails to show how this could possibly work in practice. How is a myriad of 'bottom up' detailed outcomes to be compared and judged? Sen might be right in that just institutions do not guarantee just outcomes. His conceptual- isation of justice is more bottom up than top down but he simply does not show how it could work. More importantly, Sen fails to show how reason and public reasoning necessarily promote just outcomes. He doesn't even try to establish this very necessary connection but just assumes it.

The puzzle of the Enlightenment which Sen's proposal highlights is that reason and reasonableness have no necessary link. Fascism has its own internal logic. Reason does not require or drive virtue. Ethics are arbitrary and justice is indefinable. Sen's example of the flute somewhat proves this. The base hypothesis of justice would be that the child who has made the flute owns it.

Providing that the producer child used her own materials and equipment (and Sen fails to make the crucial point that more detailed information is needed here and in every situational determination of justice), then on what possible basis can two other children who want the flute claim it from the child who made it? If the producer simply has to give the flute to another child then there are unlikely to be any more flutes made. Sen also omits any creative solutions such as sharing of the flute, training other children how to make flutes themselves etc. In the end Sen's 'Idea of Justice' fails to solve the one simple example he offers and leaves justice as an unresolved dilemma.

It is clear that there is massive inequality in the world today. Inequality of outcome but of opportunity as well. If there is doubt and debate about the equalisation of outcomes, there can surely be less or none about equalisation of opportunity. And yet children's life chances within and between countries are hugely different as a result of different educational opportunity. Justice would require that all children get a good and equal start. Justice therefore requires sacrifice of selfishness – simply maximising my children's potential without any regard for other people's children, and in some implicit way even competitively against them, does not accord with justice or with any of the other virtues that go with it. And yet that has become established middle class thinking in the UK, including and even sometimes especially so in its churches.

This is why justice requires further qualities and cannot stand as an independent mono value. Justice needs mercy. Mercy is justice's opposite but more meaningfully synthesised as its balancing virtue. Justice can be severe or it can be merciful. This is a question of choice. Justice also needs truth. Without knowing the totality of all relevant facts, and without understanding the context and nuances of these facts, justice cannot be applied, or else is applied blindly and is in danger of being an injustice itself. It is interpreted through generosity and through wisdom. But the ultimate Christian motif is that justice may only be available if injustice is sometimes carried by some who suffer it. This is the more meaningful interpretation of Christ's death, that it was unjustly borne. Not all injustice can be assuaged or corrected. There is simply too much of it around. Legal arguments and settlements to resolve it all would go on for ever. Attempts to compensate for past injustices such as slavery are bound to be incomplete. Shell shocked soldiers who were shot by their own army as deserters cannot be brought back to life. A thief cannot necessarily restore what has been stolen. So some compromise has to be reached and that requires justice's moderating virtues of generosity and mercy, as well as the grace to bear some injustice in an imperfect world in the interest of establishing a more just ongoing world. This is a more unique and a more value centred contribution of religious understandings to the concern for justice.

Love

There are huge hymns to love in the Bible, none more famous than the 1 Corinthians 13 passage frequently read at weddings (although this reading is not allowed in civil weddings in the UK). God we are told is love. God so loves the world. The greatest commandment is to love. Love is the proof of Christian discipleship. Love drives out fear. There are 35 references to love in the first short letter written by the apostle John. This is amazing, not only as a demonstration of the focus on love in Christianity's Bible, but as a further case along with justice where themes which are highly valued in secular thought and general consciousness are in fact central to religion from which society has become alienated. Even sexual love is celebrated in the Song of Songs.

As mentioned in a previous section, the Christian author C S Lewis (who incidentally pioneered the practice of a marriage of convenience by marrying an American to ensure UK health care for her), objected to the statement that love is God, insisting that the Bible said on the contrary that God is love. Well so what? Defining love as divine has widespread assent. If we are inventing our divine, love would undoubtedly be supported as an attribute. Making love divine is not some idle weak romantic poetic notion. Rather it is the strong love by which, as Jesus said, a person might lay down their life for the one they love. Making love divine is a huge commitment as it sets love as the ruling principle for life. It elevates the interests of others and challenges the self interest of the consumer society and of the purely Darwinian human being. It redefines Dawkin's selfish gene. Attempts by value Darwinists like Matt Ridley to argue that love and altruism are tools for selfish survival are too mechanistic. Making love divine is revolutionary.

Such a divine love is of a special type. The writings of the apostle John and of theologians like Anders Nygren in 'Agape and Eros' define a particular concept of love which is called 'agape' in Greek. This stands in stark distinction to eros, a love which is self gratifying. It is also differentiated from the 'philia' of friendship and the 'storge' of affection, valuable as these loves are. The fundamental difference of agape or caritas is that it is unconditional of circumstances, or of the attractiveness or behaviour of the person loved. It is self sacrificial on the part of the lover.

Just as society values justice, so it values love and especially this particular agape love.

Market

Every society has its gods and its theology. Communist society enforced atheism and banned churches, turning them into warehouses and sports halls, but then substituted worship of its leaders like Lenin whose mausoleum was still visited by hordes of pilgrims to Red Square in Moscow as recently as the 1990s. They used to get awards for being best worker in their factory, or committed local party member, and the reward was a trip to Moscow to queue in all weathers to see Lenin's embalmed corpse. It was probably the most famous disincentive ever devised. China did the same with Mao Zedong and Vietnam with Ho Chi Minh, though biographies of Ho suggest he never sought such personal adulation and was more committed to independence for Vietnam than to a communist creed.

Western public opinion is too disrespectful to worship its political leaders and so, as religious belief declined, new gods of social democracy and free market economy were enthroned. It was amazing how solid the faith in the twin deities of social democracy and free markets became. Apparently we could all switch off our brains, cognitive capability and intelligence, and let the market sort everything out for us. Not only was this free market capable of working out all complex economic issues and delivering ever increasing prosperity, but like any real god it had an angry determinative side to its nature too. Many formerly intelligent people believed that it was impossible to 'buck the market'. Government ministers and press commentators told us this. International development support largely consisted of introducing poor and developing nations on this earth to this wonderful gospel of faith in social democracy and free markets. Consultants got paid good money as evangelists for this gospel. Civil servants washed their hands of any responsibility for industrial strategy, since all that was required was to let the benign divine free market work its wonders. It was amazing to see this divine status accorded to the simple artefact of the market, to hear intelligent people expect a metaphysical entity without intelligence or moral values calculate economic outcomes which humanity had no choice but to accept, since they could not be altered. If the market produced unemployment or inequality, or despoiled the environment, or lowered wages, or geared up company balance sheets to explosion, or advanced credit to people unable to repay, then it would be self corrective through its super intelligent price signal and response mechanisms and glory would be restored.

This is clear nonsense, but like all religious nonsense it is amazing how widespread the belief became, only starting to unravel in 2008 when mega market collapse occurred. The market mechanism clearly is a helpful economic tool, but one which must stay servant and never master to humanity. It is not inviolate. Its outcomes can be adjusted, altered or rejected. Its decision processes can be monitored, influenced and changed by cognitive economic management. Classical economic theory clearly identifies points of market failure. Monopolies are one, which is why most economic law includes anti monopoly legislation to maintain competition. But the concept of competition, whilst a partial useful tool to promote efficient economic and business performance, is itself limited. Competitions get won. Industrial sectors evolve through early periods of fragmented competition to highly concentrated profiles. It is usual to see 3 firm concentration ratios in excess of 70% market share in many sectors. Consumers settle into established choices, since constant review of competitive offers can be daunting. People may switch suppliers of electrical goods using Internet consumer technology, but most people prefer to settle into shopping at a preferred, maybe local, supermarket or shop. The hassle of changing bank accounts with any frequency leads to customer loyalty even when the banks play tunes on interest rates with customer inertia.

Monopoly is not the only case of market failure. It can come through information failures too. People may simply not be aware of potential supply or demand, and therefore not act according to this potential. Price signals may be hidden. It is interesting to see how the Internet has reduced this informational imperfection and led to pricing close to the textbook model of perfect competition which assumes perfect information. Externalities is another classic failure. The market fails to include external costs, for example those of environmental pollution, in the product cost, leading to overconsumption and overproduction. Land is not included at replacement cost or even at historic cost in many family farm accounts, leading to a cost which does not include real resource cost and therefore sends the wrong price signals.

Apart from these technical economic arguments on market failure, there is an overriding moral point. Do we as intelligent cognitive responsible humans want to hand our economic outcomes to Adam Smith's blind impersonal 'hidden hand'? We may well object to this either philosophically or pragmatically because we don't like the market outcome and see that some other outcome may be preferable and possible. How free are 'free' markets? Freedom itself is a limited scarce commodity. One person's freedom is another person's constraint. For those with capability, energy, vision, contacts and funding the world may seem very free. The world is indeed their oyster. But for others lacking these blessed qualities the market may seem more of a trap than free space. Freedom is a great thing and should be maximised, not unnecessarily constrained, but the ideal that all people are created equal and born free and that this freedom is a universal reality or even opportunity is delusional. Markets can operate in freedom but they are value free and have no inbuilt ethic to respect freedom which has to be preserved and enhanced by political means.

Surprisingly this critique of market was expressed forcibly by Christ. In a powerful short story in John's gospel we read, 'In the temple courts he found men selling cattle, sheep and doves, and others sitting at table exchanging money. So he made a whip out of cords, and drove all from the temple area, both sheep and cattle ; he scattered the coins of the money-changers and overturned their tables. To those who sold doves he said 'Get these out of here! How dare you turn my father's house into a market!'' (John chapter 2 verses 14-16). This story is a very interesting demonstration of two points which converge into fresh meaning, and into a potential new shared synthesis between an atheistic society and a non doctrinal Christianity. This incident feeds no doctrinal interpretation of Christianity. It has not been extracted by the doctrinal fundamentalists and made into something you have to believe to be a Christian. It shares this doctrine free status with much else of Christ's thought, sayings, actions, parables and story. As such it shows the total inadequacy of the doctrinal interpretation, the ABC of faith, the 39 articles of the Church of England, or any work of systematic theology to capture Christian meaning. It stands independent of any such simplistic doctrinal manipulation and conveys its own significance. Secondly that significance is shared by probably a majority of today's secular population who are uncomfortable with, or in straightforward opposition to, the prevalence of market concepts throughout life including areas which should be 'holy' from market and its blunt instruments of money, price, profit and loss. Today health and education are markets. Schools and hospitals, teachers and surgeons have to compete for consumers who can choose between them. Many would think that this is a step too far for market mechanisms. There are in many people's eyes things in life, like love, like family, which are too precious to be measured by price. Children's lives and the education of those lives may well be included in that holy preserve. We may well say something similar to Christ at this point and ask how dare you turn this into a market?

So we have a cogent example of the synthesis this book is seeking to explore. No belief at all is required to get value and meaning from this temple/market story. In fact it is incapable of being processed or interpreted by belief. No belief in God, in the deity of Christ, in the Bible as the word of God is needed or indeed even relevant or helpful. Everyone can take this story, this morality play, and value its point. Society may well find value enhancement from it if it led to policies which regarded market as servant and not demigod. Whether secular atheist society can drop its prejudice to access such texts, and whether church can be persuaded to drop its false claim to ownership and doctrinal interpretation of the same text to allow a new synthesis to develop, is the core question for the hope of this book.

Institutions

The market is one example of the wide class of institutions which govern human life. Like the market, other institutions can also grow to dominate and rule rather than serve humanity which created them in the first place. Once established they become set in concrete and inflexible, failing then to meet the need they were initially conceived for. The set of institutions is wide and includes the law, democracy, established practices, marriage, the family, institutions and offices of state. Institutions are the software of human society. They enable interaction and social life. This ranges from simple institutions or protocols like a handshake for greeting and parting which has morphed into a hug or a kiss in some cultures, through simple traffic rules, to a wide range of procedures as to how we all agree to go about life together. Without such institutions, every interaction would require re-invention of a procedure every time we wanted to do anything.

Take the example of a friendship. Two friends may realise that without some determined deliberate organisation the pace of their lives means they may see each other very rarely. So they institute a regular pattern of meeting. It may be once a week or once a year but nevertheless it has become an institution. At its initiation this institution serves their needs, is servant to the friends and to their friendship. But as time goes on life proves again to be dynamic. Their interests diverge, one may move to a distant town to live, the other may have suddenly increased responsibilities. They find that they have less in common and the meetings become a burden rather than a joy. At this stage they probably need to change their institution and agree to meet less often, or perhaps even not at all except if some special occasion arises.

Failure to evolve institutions means that they change their status from servant to master. Because institutions are themselves inorganic, ie lifeless and without intelligence, feeling or awareness, they do fail to evolve unless the humans who initiated them change them. But here lies the rub. People initially institute institutions to act as an enabling infrastructure to life and so they follow and obey them. To change them is antithetical to the whole idea of institution. This reluctance to change and evolve institutions, since they are incapable of changing or evolving themselves, leaves humanity with a master which can become a monster. The creature, the created artefact, dictates to its creator. This, as we have seen, can be true of the institution of the market. But it can also be true of a wide range of institutions.

Even the law can either become outdated, can fail to represent current ethics as ethics evolve, or indeed can be miscalculated in the sense of having unforeseen and unwanted consequences in some combination of situations. For this reason the law itself is not absolute, but has to be refined and redefined as a constant dynamic. It is not very long ago that the law condemned homosexuals to imprisonment, as in the case of Oscar Wilde, and not long before that when it publicly executed gay people. Today, as has already been pointed out, the law prevents a Roman Catholic from becoming sovereign in the UK. This law is unacceptable in a pluralist tolerant society and indeed contradicts other laws against religious discrimination. Nevertheless the government takes the view that changing this law would be too complex so the created law acts as a dictator against the wishes of the society that created it. The law is as blind, as unintelligent and as unfeeling as the market. Both are inorganic dead artefacts. Both are needed for the regular conduct of human life but both should be servant to cognitive human masters.

Institutions often operate through organisations whose complex dynamics are well analysed in Etzione's famous 'Complex Organisations'. The church itself is a very rigid inflexible institution. It continues with anachronistic practices of distinguishing and dividing clergy from lay people, dressing clergy druidically, preaching at people - all from a day when the clergy were the few literate members of the population. Its rituals range from waving hands in the air ecstatically through sacraments of baptism and communion of bread and wine to kissing icons. It avoids dialogue, challenge or debate. It is one of the most unilateral of institutions. It apparently finds it impossible to evolve.

When institutions fail to adapt to human developments, two outcomes are possible, depending on relative power. If the institution has power it can survive unscathed. In this case the small group of people who benefit from the institution, for example by maintaining influential or well paid roles, will be pleased, but the vast majority of people who now want a different regime will lose out, sometimes severely. If on the other hand the reform movement has greater power, then the institution will either wither or die. The church has done both in parts. Whilst it has admittedly flourished in very small niche interest groups, for example the social elite class of London stockbrokers desperately in need of release from emotional sclerosis who find charismatic Anglican church practices appealing, in general it has withered on its own vine. It has continued with its anachronistic practices, has been proved wrong on every question from Copernicus to evolution to evolving sexual ethics, and yet neither invites nor welcomes any debate with those it is pompous enough to 'mission' to. As a consequence it has remained unchanged on an isolated island of sadly increasing irrelevance. Institutions are not organic and this failure to evolve means that reality moves on and away from them.

Organisations need structures and these structures themselves become institutionalised. Power brokers know this and use the structure of the institution to create at worst social monsters, as demagogues of the likes of Stalin, Saddam Hussein, Idi Amin and Pol Pot have done. But milder forms of abuse of institutional structure occur almost inevitably and endemically.

Organisations define roles for people. Most people are only able to fulfil their careers and carry out their working lives through roles allocated to them in organisations, whether these are commercial companies, government departments or non governmental organisations. Rarely are roles created for people. Roles are themselves institutions and share the same sclerosis. A role is usually initially created to recognise, define and therefore enable the work contribution of a specific person in a specific context. For example the role of President of the United States was created in 1789 and occupied by George Washington. But this same role has subsequently been occupied by 43 other people in a very wide variety of contexts for American society. If the definition of the role has no room for flexibility then it will not be optimal for all new presidents in all new contexts. On the other hand, there are people who operate outside given roles within predefined organisations. Society needs these people operating in new non institutional streams as they are an important symbiotic dynamic alongside the static of the major institutions. They enable change. Often they have to found their own new institutions. All these are examples of how institutions, organisations and the structures, roles and procedures they create need to be responsive to the dynamic context of human life.

The Jewish Sabbath is an example of a rigid static institution. Very many restrictions on activity turn what was intended to be a time of restoration and relaxation into a day of rigor mortis. Jesus was challenged by the Sabbath observation society because he and his disciples were eating corn they had picked from a field. Only dire religion can even think of prohibiting such a natural and simple joy. Jesus replied with a phrase of great and generic insight – 'Man was not made for the Sabbath but the Sabbath for man'. All institutions should serve rather than rule.

There is an unavoidable trade off here. We need institutions as a framework which sets our procedures or else we would never know how to go about anything, but we also need them to adapt. On the other hand, too frequent adaptation can turn out to be expensive and confusing. Striking the right point to create flexible adaptive institutions is a major challenge but one which should always be in open debate. Christ's saying on the subject is profound and is another example of how secular society can gain insight from its religious texts.

The role of the state

Life requires institutions including the institution of government. How pervasive that government should be is a question which has differentiated societies through history. American society champions the concept of the small state with maximum personal liberty and entrepreneurial responsibility. UK society shifted from a more statist to a more entrepreneurial society with the election of the Thatcher government in 1979, whilst French and German social models remained more communal and their economic policy more *dirigiste*. Asiatic societies tend towards more heavy handed or at least more patronising government – the Singapore government once took out adverts telling its citizens not to take too much food at buffet lunches but to let the world know that Singaporeans are polite!

Franz Kafka depicted the grim reality of totalitarian government in his classic work 'The Trial', set in an eastern European society in the early twentieth century. The Soviet Union controlled a huge totality of life with the economy planned in detail by Gosplan, private initiative proscribed, and detailed individual action subject to state scrutiny. Kafka was a determined pessimist – even in his novel 'America', the promised land of individual freedom turns out to be a delusion. The free market can also trap, enslave and impoverish people just as John Steinbeck similarly portrays it in his 'Grapes of Wrath'.

In answer to a trick question, Christ offers another insightful saying. He is asked whether taxes should be paid to the occupying Roman government, and he asks for a coin for illustration, asking whose face was on it, to which his questioners replied 'Caesar's'. 'Render to Caesar the things that are Caesar's and to God the things that are God's' he replied in Mark chapter 12 verse 16. It's a classic saying which has stood the test of time and still has current meaning and significance. Again it is not necessary to believe in any doctrine about the person of Christ to savour the meaning of this powerful succinct saying. It is a political philosophy in a phrase. Just as he limited the role of the market in human life by ejecting it from life's holy core, so he limits the role of government and of the state. There are things, less meaningful things he implies such as money, which are in the purvey of the state, but other things which are clearly not.

Christ's definition of God here is the protection and preservation of core areas of human life which do not belong to the state. They are a holy preserve and no state has rightful access. England's Queen Elizabeth the First rightly resolved in Francis Bacon's words 'not to make windows into men's hearts and secret thoughts'. Again this message is joy to the hearts of all civil rights movements and is embraced and endorsed by them. It is a theological message, but does not require doctrinal belief in an exogenous God. It is another example of a component of synthesis where church and secular society might find themselves closer together if the church adopted wider intellectual and less simplistic doctrinal interpretations.

Myth – and resurrection

It is paradoxical that literal beliefs answer the 'so what?' question far less meaningfully than mythical interpretations. Christians believe in the virgin birth of Christ. With all due respect to those who hold it dear, this belief fails to answer the 'so what' question at all. It might suggest the idea of the unworthiness of human sex and reproduction, which is a rather morbid interpretation and bolsters already negative and damaged views of sexuality. When once asked by a senior Russian communist industrialist to explain the why? of the virgin birth I struggled and failed, realising myself that there hardly was any meaningful meaning. The belief is in any case shrouded in mystery – was divine semen implanted or a formed foetus? It really makes little sense. On the other hand the same hardy communist was most moved by the story of the resurrection of Christ and immediately saw its significance. This is typical of Russian Orthodoxy whose strands may still have permeated his awareness despite its severe repression under the communist regime. For Russian Orthodoxy, resurrection is more important than crucifixion, whereas for Protestant Christians it's almost the other way round since they place such extraordinary theological emphasis on the death of Christ.

On one occasion the American evangelist Billy Graham invited a Russian Orthodox priest to accompany him on this preaching schedule and to offer comment. The Russian priest complimented Graham on his talks which he had clearly found more enlightened than he had expected, but made this point that a Russian Orthodox Christian would put much more emphasis on the resurrection than on the crucifixion. One of Tolstoy's great novels is entitled 'Resurrection' and the Russian word for Sunday 'voskresyeniya' also means resurrection.

But the question is what is being believed here. Western evangelical Christians insist that a literal resurrection of a physical body is an essential litmus test of Christian belief. If you don't believe this you are not a Christian. But why? And what's the point? Believing in a bodily resurrection seems rather pointless, given that there is no body whose absence then has to be explained by a subsequent 'ascension'. The only outcome then is to believe in the spiritual aspects of this resurrection. The Christian belief is that the Spirit came to replace Christ on earth, but this Spirit is invisible and therefore non incarnate. The resurrection has therefore become Gnostic. Indeed insisting on a bodily resurrection and deriding the concept of spiritual resurrection as 'Gnostic' seems pointless when the bodily resurrection was itself such a short lived and temporary phenomenon.

We can get to a very similar outcome by another route. To some it will be heresy to claim that belief in the physical resurrection of Christ has less implication than embracing the myth of resurrection. The onus is then on them to say what the implication of believing in the literal bodily resurrection is. Is it victory over death? The 'O death where is thy victory, o grave where is thy sting' of 1 Corinthians 15? But death remains, often in agonising ways, and any victory over it is relegated to an afterlife which becomes a necessary adjunct to derive meaning from the literal interpretation of resurrection. In any case, the claimed literal resurrection of Christ as of Lazarus was not in an afterlife but back to contemporary life.

On the other hand the myth of resurrection has huge interpretative potential. Christ himself makes use of this myth interpretation when he says in John chapter 12 verse 24, 'Unless a grain of wheat falls into the ground and dies, it remains alone. But if it dies, it produces a lot of grain'. This offers a wide range of heuristic, enlightening, meaningful and applicable interpretations, which is more than can be said for the literal interpretation of resurrection. For example hope can ever arise out of despair, fresh joy from depths of sorrow. Failed initiatives can generate new and maybe different sprouting. It is worth forgoing consumption now to invest to build for tomorrow. A new dawn sees the sun resurrected daily, spring resurrects dormant plant life. And we as human beings can find the resurrections in this life which regenerate. Loved ones who have passed away would not want mourning to suppress our lives for ever thereafter but would rejoice to see our joy resurrected so that in this sense at least death is not victorious.

Here is one major example where myth has greater power than literalism. We can reasonably and justifiably claim that the very extensive use of parables by Christ in his discourse makes myth more central to Christianity than literal beliefs, some of which, like literal belief in the Trinity, have caused more havoc than peace, more confusion than enlightenment, and more heat than light.

Myth - the trinity

This doctrine of the Trinity exemplifies why doctrine is a less satisfactory interpretation than myth. There has been immense theological dispute about this doctrine, including disputes leading to violence and death, so that it has a net negative contribution to humanity to date. No-one understands it. The church insists on it, but cannot explain it. There are three separate persons in one godhead. They are co-equal, co-eternal etc. It is a mystery, young initiates are told. Neither does it have any measurable significance. It is an imposition without value. The Oxford Dictionary of the Christian Church defines The Trinity as the central dogma of Christian theology, even though the word never appears in the Bible, which means that the church invented the idea or at best synthesised it from various Bible hints and then proceeded to enforce it and make it a requirement of faith. There is of course dissent and Binitarians and Unitarians abound. But for most people it's an incomprehensible irrelevance.

At this point we might as well scrap or ignore it except that, unusually for him, the apostle Paul offers a myth/meaning interpretation. In his famous 'grace' in 2 Corinthians chapter 13 verse 14 he writes 'The grace of the Lord Jesus Christ, and the love of

God, and the fellowship of the Holy Spirit, be with you all'. Here we have a presentation of this trinity in terms of their meaning. God means love, Christ means grace, and the Holy Spirit means fellowship. These meanings are more important than belief in any literal persons of the godhead. Who would not want a life and human society characterised by grace and love? Indeed the wish expressed in the grace is that the resulting fellowship would be universal, would be 'with you all'.

Suddenly the trinity is interpreted to convey a very attractive idea, rather than a meaningless dogma. The idea is not just an appealing description of an unreachable state of bliss but offers some causal connectivity, ie a way to get there too. 'Fellowship' is an old fashioned religious word although it is also preserved in its use for some professional and academic groups. It can be translated as 'communion' but that is an equally quaint dated word. It conveys the idea of a harmonious relationship, either between two people or a wider group. It includes mutual aid, acceptance and is entirely positive in its connotations. It is inclusive but not exclusive. It can be 'with you all' and in fact is quintessentially inclusive to the point of universality. It doesn't have entrance criteria but it does have self defining membership characteristics, those of grace and love. Grace and love lead to fellowship. This is the trinity of meaning. Human disharmony is due to the absence of either or both. The 'agape' self giving love celebrated in the section above needs no doctrine, no belief and no church. Where it characterises life and interaction it generates the wonder of fellowship. This principle is obvious in one sense, is definitely universal in application, but is little recognised or vocalised in contemporary society, which is more oriented to selfish pursuit than to self giving love.

The Pauline grace deserves to be re-established more as poetry rather than as theology. Grace is a word which has almost fallen out of common use. It has been relegated to a religious word meaning 'undeserved favour'. Protestants who seem to rejoice in conflict and controversy and adversarial thinking compare it unfavourably to 'works'. Their main idea is that human good deeds are irrelevant and cannot gain merit so that we all need God's grace. This achieves the amazing self contradiction of a non gracious interpretation of grace. Physical movement as in ballet can have a grace. So can behaviour. To be gracious does embrace being kind, polite, generous, forgiving, encouraging, merciful, compassionate. Grace is the characteristic which generates these virtues. It is easy to see how and why it joins with agape love to yield fellowship. The Greek words for this trinity are agape, charis and koinonia - they possess something of an onomatopoeic quality, their gentle sound suggesting their content.

In this discourse we have secularised the trinity, stripped it of persons of a godhead, and in so doing rendered it comprehensible, accessible and maybe desirable to secular human beings. This typifies the synthesis between sacred and secular, between church and society, between atheism and faith which is the mission of this book. The best concept of greeting a secular revolution has ever brought is 'bonjour citoyen'. How poor in meaning compared to this divine trinity - 'grace and love and fellowship be with everyone'.

Myth - sibling rivalry

An opening Bible story in Genesis chapter 4 is that of Cain and Abel, sons of Adam and Eve. Cain is a farmer and Abel a shepherd. Abel gets into greater favour for the meat he provides. Cain gets jealous and angry and murders Abel. God challenges Cain before the murder. The challenge is that there is no need for sibling jealousy and invidious comparison because each can do well. But Cain is driven by his jealousy and yields to it rather than mastering it, which according to God he could have done. The resulting murder leads to the famous curse on Cain that he will be a wandering farmer in arduous conditions, but the curse is moderated to protect him from random murder. It's clear that the story became archetypal since it is referred to by three New Testament writers.

Sibling rivalry is a very common phenomenon and it's no exaggeration to say that it often brings its own curse. Parents can sometimes be unwise in the way they praise or provide differentially for each of two or more children. Once sown in a young heart, sibling rivalry is hard to dislodge and can have lifelong destructive consequences. The same opportunity is offered to all who face its ugly possibility or reality - there is no need for it since every child can do well on their own terms, absolutely rather than relatively. Such self acceptance deeply rooted rids the mind of jealousy and the hatred it can generate. The story of Cain and Abel doesn't have to come from the Bible. It could come as any ancient fable and still retain its interpretative power. It is another example of the power religious literature can offer without needing to demand any belief in anything literal or in any doctrine. The content is valuable and unthreatening and so there is no need to reject it, just as there is no need to slavishly regard it as the authoritative word of God.

Fear

Fear is pervasive in human beings and in human society. An immense range of 'phobias' are defined which destabilise life for many. Even opposites like agoraphobia and claustrophobia cause fear in different people. People can be afraid of the past or the future. Many fear the dark. Behavioural compensation for fear can also be the opposites of withdrawal or aggression. Religion is often considered to be fearful and to play on people's fears. But true religion recognises and assuages fear. There are two potentially helpful expressions in the Bible concerning fear. One in the Old Testament is in Psalm 23 which states 'though I walk through the valley of the shadow of death I will fear no evil'. The other in the New Testament is from 1 John chapter 4 verse 18 which says 'there is no fear in love but perfect love casts out fear'. Once again we have valuable poetry which requires no doctrinal belief and does not even fit into any doctrinal construct. It is worth free reflection. Firstly, because whatever the gravity of any situation, it is possible not to let fear dominate. Fear can in fact be self fulfilling and this destructive cycle is best broken. The second concept gives some suggestion as to how this might happen. Love in life is effective in getting rid of fears. People who love and who are loved show greater quiet inner security and less fear. These ideas are not prescriptive or simplistically automatic but they are heuristic. Thoughts on fear are another example of how a non doctrinaire approach to religious literature can be worthwhile.

The blessed life

I cite here two Bible passages, one from the Old Testament and one from the New. The first is Psalm 23, recognised for the beauty of its sentiment by often being read at funerals. It is however more a song of life than one of death. Here it is

> The Lord is my shepherd, I shall not be in want
> He makes me lie down in green pastures
> He leads me beside quiet waters
> He restores my soul
> He guides me in paths of justice for his name's sake
>
> Even though I walk through the valley of the shadow of death
> I will fear no evil

For you are with me, your rod and your staff they comfort me

You prepare a table before me in the presence of my enemies
You anoint my head with oil, my cup overflows

Surely goodness and love will follow me all the days of my
life
and I will dwell in the house of the Lord forever

The second is the 'blessed' sayings of Jesus in his famed 'sermon
on the mount' in Matthew chapter 5. Here they are

Blessed are the poor in spirit for theirs is the kingdom of
heaven
Blessed are those who mourn for they shall be comforted
Blessed are the meek for they shall inherit the earth
Blessed are those who hunger and thirst for justice for they
will be filled
Blessed are the merciful for they shall be shown mercy
Blessed are the pure in heart for they will see God
Blessed are the peacemakers for they will be called sons of
God
Blessed are those who are persecuted because of justice for
theirs is the kingdom of heaven

It's clear that these passages hang around a statement of God.
But does this mean that they are only available or only
meaningful through doctrinal belief in God or personal
experience of God? 'No' has to be the answer because the whole
meaning of both expressions is neither to start from or to drive
towards any requirement of faith in God. Whilst they may be
addressed to those who do believe in God, and therefore whilst
they assume some God belief, they are not limited to a God
perspective. Their meaning, their value expression, their poetry,

their inspiration and beauty can validly be extracted by anyone with any or no belief, like taking honey from the honeycomb despite the bees who claim exclusive ownership and try to sting and inhibit entry.

This is particularly possible once we have replaced an exogenous God by an endogenous divine in the way suggested earlier in this book. Those who do believe in God have no problem. They have access. But they do not have exclusive ownership, either they, or their belief interpretation, or their church. The problem is not access for God believers, but access for those who for reasons worked through in much recent literature simply cannot believe in God. Theirs may still be this kingdom, the myth kingdom of justice, of love, of mercy, of comfort, of a restored soul, of an overflowing life, of purity of heart. Because myth is stronger than doctrine since it has greater implication.

If a simple experience like a glorious day or a wonderful meal can be described as divine, if to forgive is divine, then the poetry of these two texts is certainly divine. Divine poetry which can be not only inspirational but also formative to the human soul. No strings are attached, no conditions are enforced. It is freely available unconditionally. Its interpretation is personal and each personal interpretation is deeply valid, uniquely precious to the beholder and subject to no critique or denial by any other agency.

If we choose to acknowledge our own construct and concept of what we regard as divine, if we enthrone justice as god, an idea which many may readily be persuaded of and to which we may eagerly subscribe, then we have a shepherd in life, a guiding principle which brings with it the peaceful fulfilled life, untroubled by fear of any kind including fear of evil. Common paranoia and pervasive enmity fade away. Life feels and is enabled. Every day is characterised by goodness. Mercy prevails in attitudes and interactions. Love is constant. Big shot celebrities no longer fill the screen of our consciousness and dominate human society, but humility is restored as a virtue. Truth is valued and is a rule, and its liberating quality is released. Great! Do we need God for this? No. We can grasp the divine values without any God belief. We can become disciples of values. Not only our life but also our world will be better for it. No-one and no institution can own, dictate or define this discipleship for us. It is ours, for each person to find, to define for themselves, to treasure and to live by.

Hosting the synthesis

How can such a synthesis be expressed, developed, shared, defined, incarnated? Today's church would have to change its emphasis and pre-conditions substantially to be able to fulfil a host role. This might not be impossible. For example in the communist German Democratic Republic, the Lutheran church played host to the reform movement which eventually led to regime change. Hyman Maccoby, writing of Jewish faith structures, identifies the temple as the regime but the synagogue as a place of sympathetic counsel and thought. After the second world war, the German church instituted its 'Kirchentag', a movement dedicated to work against any recurrence of fascism by its commitment to the priority of personal conscience above state dictat, the Bible as a source of spiritual inspiration, and the inclusion of the outsider. Kirchentag's bi-annual city wide events do succeed in bringing secular and sacred together in debate and action. Church therefore is one possible host for developing of a synthesis which does not insist on specific or any belief, but it will have to be prepared to be servant rather than master – a role exchange it has rarely shown itself ready to accept.

Bibliography

Anderson, P. *The Origins of Postmodernity*, Verso, 1998

Armstrong, K. *The Bible*, Atlantic, 2008

Armstrong, K. *Islam A Short History*, Orion, 2001

Armstrong, K. *The Battle for God*, HarperCollins, 2001

Baggini, J. *What's it all about? Philosophy and the Meaning of Life*, Granta, 2005

Beasley-Murray, G. R. *Jesus and the Kingdom of God*, Eerdmans, 1986

Berkhof, L. *Systematic Theology*, Banner of Truth, 1971

Berlin, I. *The Crooked Timber of Humanity*, Vintage, 2003

Berlin, I. *The Proper Study of Mankind*, Vintage, 1998

Berlin, I. *Against the Current*, Vintage, 1997

Berman, M. *All that is Solid Melts into the Air*, Verso, 1993

Blackburn, S. *Think*, Oxford, 2001

Blackburn, S. *Being Good*, Oxford, 2002

Boenhoeffer, D. *The Cost of Discipleship*, SCM, 2001

Bohm, D. *Causality and Chance in Modern Physics*, Routledge, 1984

Bowler, P. *Evolution – The History of an Idea*, University of California, 2009

Carson, R. *Silent Spring*, Penguin, 1965

Chalke, S. *The Lost Message of Jesus*, Zondervan, 2004

Comte-Sponville, A. *The Little Book of Philosophy*, Heinemann, 2004

Comte-Sponville, A. *The Book of Atheist Spirituality*, Bantam, 2008

Comte-Sponville, A. *A Short Treatise on the Great Virtues*, Heinemann, 2002

Crick, F. *The Astonishing Hypothesis*, Simon and Schuster, 1995

Cushing, J. *Philosophical Concepts in Physics*, Cambridge, 2003

Darwin, C. *The Origin of Species*, Penguin, 1985

Davies, P. *The Goldilocks Enigma*, Penguin, 2007

Dawkins, R. *The Selfish Gene*, Oxford, 2006

Dawkins, R. *The Blind Watchmaker*, Penguin, 2006

Dawkins, R. *The God Delusion*, Transworld, 2007

Doxiadis, A. et al *Logicomix*, Bloomsbury, 2009

Dupre, L. *Enlightenment and the Intellectual Foundations of Modern Culture*, Yale, 2004

Eagleton, T. *Reason, Faith, and Revolution*, Yale, 2009

Etzione, A. *A Comparative Analysis of Complex Organisations*, Free Press, 1971

Etzione, A. *New Communitarian Thinking: Persons, Virtues, Institutions and Communities*, University of Virginia, 1995

Fernandez-Aremesto, F. *Millennium: A History of our Last Thousand Years*, Bantam, 1995

Fernandez-Aremesto, F. *Ideas that Changed the World*, Dorling Kindersley, 2003

Fernandez-Aremesto, F. *Civilisations*, Macmillan, 2000

Fernandez-Aremesto, F. *So You Think You're Human*, Oxford, 2005

Flew, A. *There is a God*, HarperOne, 2008

Follesdal, D. *Quine in Dialogue*, Harvard University Press, 2008

Harvey, D. *The Condition of Postmodernity*, Blackwell, 1991

Hawthorne, N. *Scarlet Letter*, Oxford, 2009

Hawthorne, N. *The Birthmark*, Oxford, 2009

Hill, C. *The English Bible and the Seventeenth Century Revolution*, Penguin, 1994

Himmelfarb, G. *The Roads to Modernity*, Vintage, 2008

Holloway, R. *Between the Monster and the Saint*, Canongate, 2008

Holloway, R. *Looking in the Distance*, Canongate, 2004

Holloway, R. *On Forgiveness*, Canongate, 2002

Holloway, R. *Doubts and Loves*, Canongate, 2003

Holloway, R. *Godless Morality*, Canongate, 2000

Hugo, V. *Les Miserables*, Vintage, 2008

Hume, D. *Dialogues Concerning Natural Religion*, Wilder, 2008

Hume, D. *An Enquiry Concerning Human Understanding*, Oxford, 2008

Humphrys, J. *In God We Doubt*, Hodder and Stoughton, 2007

Israel, J. *Enlightenment Contested*, Oxford, 2008

Israel, J. *Radical Enlightenment*, Oxford, 2002

Kafka, F. *The Trial*, Penguin, 2000

Kafka, F. *America*, Vintage, 1998

Kierkegaard, S. *Fear and Trembling*, Penguin, 1985

King, I. *How to Make Good Decisions and Be Right All the Time*, Continuum, 2008

Lee, H. *To Kill a Mockingbird*, Vintage, 2007

Lennox, J. *God's Undertaker – Has Science Buried God?*, Lion, 2007

Lilla, M. *The Legacy of Isaiah Berlin*, New York Review of Books, 2001

Louden, R. *The World We Want*, Oxford, 2007

Loux, M. *Metaphysics*, Taylor and Francis, 2008

Loux, M. *Metaphysics - Contemporary Readings*, Routledge, 2008

Loux, M. and Zimmerman, D. *The Oxford Handbook of Metaphysics*, Oxford, 2005

Ludlow, P. *There's Something about Mary*, MIT, 2004

Maccoby, H. *The Mythmaker - Paul and the Invention of Christianity*, Barnes and Noble, 1998

MacCulloch, D. *Reformation - Europe's House Divided*, Penguin, 2004

MacCulloch, D. *A History of Christianity*, Penguin, 2009

Neiman, S. *Moral Clarity*, Bodley Head, 2009

Nietzsche, F. *Beyond Good and Evil*, Penguin, 2003

Nozick, R. *Anarchy, State and Utopia*, Basic Books, 1977

Anders N., *Agape and Eros*, HarperCollins, 1969

Paley, W. *Natural Theology*, Oxford, 2008

Plato, *The Republic*, Penguin, 2007

Popper, K. *The Logic of Scientific Discovery*, Routledge, 2002

Popper, K. *A World of Propensities*, Thoemmes, 1990

Porter, R. *Flesh in the Age of Reason*, Penguin, 2004

Porter, R. *Enlightenment*, Penguin, 2000

Racevskis, K. *Postmodernism and the Search for Enlightenment*, University of Virginia, 1993

Rawls, J. *A Theory of Justice*, Harvard University Press, 1999

Ricks, C. *T S Eliot and Prejudice*, Faber and Faber, 1994

Ridley, M. *The Origins of Virtue*, Penguin, 1997

Robertson, J. *The Case for the Enlightenment*, Cambridge, 2007

Rosenberg, N. *Technology and the Wealth of Nations*, Stanford, 1992

Russell, B. *History of Western Philosophy*, Taylor and Francis, 2004

Sen, A. *The Idea of Justice*, Penguin, 2009

Shapiro, S. *The Oxford Handbook of Philosophy of Mathematics and Logic*, Oxford, 2007

Shapiro, S. *Thinking About Mathematics*, Oxford, 2000

Shapiro, S. *The Objectivity of Mathematics*, Synthese, 2007

Spong, J. *Why Christianity Must Change or Die*, HarperCollins, 1999

Spong, J. *A New Christianity for a New World*, HarperCollins, 2002

Spong, J. *Jesus for the Non Religious*, HarperCollins, 2007

Steinbeck, J. *The Grapes of Wrath*, Penguin, 2000

Taylor, K. *Cruelty - Human Evil and the Human Brain*, Oxford, 2009

Tolstoy, L. *Resurrection*, Penguin, 1973

Tressel, R. *The Ragged Trousered Philanthropists*, Zed, 2003

Twain, M. *Huckleberry Finn*, Random House, 2007

Vattimo, .G. *Belief*, Blackwell, 1999

Vattimo, G. *The End of Modernity*, John Hopkins, 1991

von Uexkuell, T. *Psychosomatic Medicine*, Lippincott, 1997

Yolton, J. *The Blackwell Companion to the Enlightenment*, Blackwell, 1991

Zeldin, T. *An Intimate History of Humanity*, Vintage, 1995

The Bible

BOOKS

O is a symbol of the world, of oneness and unity. In different cultures it also means the "eye," symbolizing knowledge and insight. We aim to publish books that are accessible, constructive and that challenge accepted opinion, both that of academia and the "moral majority."

Our books are available in all good English language bookstores worldwide. If you don't see the book on the shelves ask the bookstore to order it for you, quoting the ISBN number and title. Alternatively you can order online (all major online retail sites carry our titles) or contact the distributor in the relevant country, listed on the copyright page.

See our website www.o-books.net for a full list of over 500 titles, growing by 100 a year.

And tune in to myspiritradio.com for our book review radio show, hosted by June-Elleni Laine, where you can listen to the authors discussing their books.

MySpiritRadio